All About

by Dan Fitzgibbon

DECORATIONS BY DAVID MARSHALL

ATHENEUM · New York · 1984

Your Money

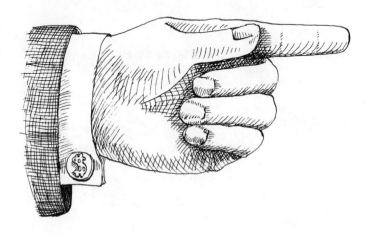

Library of Congress Cataloging in Publication Data
Fitzgibbon, Dan.   All about your money.

  Summary: Discusses the function and importance of money
and how to manage personal finances including such topics as
saving, investing, checking accounts, credit cards, borrowing
and lending.
  1. Finance, Personal.   2. Youth—Finance, Personal.
3. Money. [1. Finance, Personal.   2. Money]   I. Title.
HG179.F535   1984   332.024   83-15608
ISBN 0-689-31031-5

Text copyright © 1984 by Dan Fitzgibbon
Illustrations copyright © 1984 by Atheneum Publishers
All rights reserved
Published simultaneously in Canada by
McClelland & Stewart, Ltd.
Composition by Dix Type Inc., Syracuse, New York
Printed and bound by Fairfield Graphics,
Fairfield, Pennsylvania
Designed by Mary Ahern
First Edition

Contents

All About Your Money

Introduction

All About Your Money is a simplified introduction to the complicated world of money matters. It will show you how to earn, save, invest, manage, budget, and spend your money wisely and well. It's a book full of common sense suggestions, ideas, possibilities, and ways to make your money go further, from your first allowance to your first paycheck. It's also a book about people's attitudes toward money, developing confidence in money matters, and managing your money instead of your money managing you. It will show you how easy it is to start your own savings account, plan a weekly allowance with your parents, or how to go about finding a good-paying part-time job. And, you'll discover the pitfalls of borrowing and lending money.

Paying attention to where your money goes, how you spend it (or misspend it) can help you see what changes might make your budget or allowance go even farther. You'll learn why it's better to gain some experience in establishing a budget (and sticking to it) rather than using the shut-your-eyes-and-cross-your-fingers method of handling your money needs.

By following some of the suggestions in this book, you'll discover how your money can make money, where to keep your money, and how to deal with those big financial institutions that look so forbidding.

Cash in your pocket has a nice feeling, but what about cashless money. Learn all about charge accounts, credit cards, and their penalties and privileges. You'll also find hints on how to bargain with your parents when you find that your weekly allowance just won't get you through the week any more. This book will tell you where to keep your money and why piggy banks and bottom dresser drawers don't help your money grow.

Don't think that just because your allowance is small or your needs simple that this book is a waste of time. You already know that your money needs are going to grow right along with you, and sooner or later you are going to have to get involved in your own finances. Why not start now instead of waiting until your limited funds or your outright poverty make you hurt all over.

It's your money. And it's far better, more freeing, and definitely more satisfying to learn how to handle it yourself than to have other people do it for you. Learn how to have a healthy respect for your money and how to spend it well for your own enjoyment. Certainly money isn't everything in life (although some people do have some strange ideas about money), but a little early wisdom just might save you from a lot of grief over the next fifty years.

1

Why All the Fuss About Money

Like so many other people, somewhere in your early years you probably discovered that the subject of money did strange things to your parents and other family members. Maybe you were present when one of your parents uttered such time honored words as:

"It may come as a shock to you but money doesn't grow on trees."

"Just because we live pretty well doesn't mean we have an endless supply of money."

"If you keep this up it will drive us to the poorhouse."

Sometimes there was a lot of fuss and tension that went with these words. And over time you discovered that —for whatever the reasons—money was a pretty important element, not to be treated lightly or frivolously.

You also began to notice that money serves a number of essential purposes:

☞ It's the primary means of getting your material needs met—whether it's a hamburger, a new sweater, a used car or film for your camera.

☞ Money can enable you to participate in some of the fun, enjoyment and good times of life. Although you can have plenty of fun without spending money, much of today's entertainment and good times requires an expenditure of money.

☞ Having your own money gives you a sense of independence and freedom. No longer are you tied to what others want to do or want for you. You can follow some of your own interests and act on your own wishes—a very nice feeling.

Money to Live On

It's a pretty basic fact that people need money to live on. Unless you are planning to live in a monastery or become a modern day Robinson Crusoe, you can expect to live in a world where money is the principal means of exchange for goods and services. And since it's highly unlikely that America will revert to a swap and barter form of economy, it might be helpful to learn a bit about handling money; including earning it, saving it and spending it.

Sooner or later you will be expected to be responsible for the basics of your life including:

☞ Food

☞ Clothing

☞ Shelter

☞ Transportation

Whether you are rich or poor you are going to need money for these basic needs and for your other day to day requirements. So that's what some of the fuss is about, having the money to pay for the primary needs. And if there is only a limited amount of money available, most people figure it's best to take care of the basic needs first. There are, however, some people who get in trouble because they prefer to spend their limited funds on nonessentials. And if you suddenly find yourself without enough money to live, you may discover that the world isn't particularly sympathetic to your needs.

Money for Fun

Everyone enjoys a good time, and the world around us is just filled with many forms of entertainment to enrich our lives and give us an extra bit of pleasure. Unfortunately, most of today's pleasures have a price tag —even if it's only the cost of a movie ticket or a voluntary contribution to a museum. It seems as if the entertainment industry, the local pizza parlor and fast food burger palace have all conspired to get a share of your entertainment budget.

True, many of life's pleasures are still free, but as you move through life you'll probably discover that your tastes change and the kinds of fun you are attracted to can become amazingly expensive. Somehow a simple game of tag football gives way to an evening at a rock concert and a day's swim at the local pool is replaced by a weekend visit to your girlfriend at a summer resort.

Whatever the nature of your enjoyment, whether you do it alone or with a group of friends you can look forward to much of your entertainment:

☞ Becoming more and more costly

☞ Involving transportation

☞ Requiring expensive equipment (skis, stereo set, automobile)

Even the spartan long-distance runner requires fifty-dollar running shoes to engage in his or her favorite sport.

Money for Independence

Money also provides a more personal benefit. Having your own money, no matter how it is obtained, except perhaps armed robbery or petty theft, can give you a sense of independence and freedom. It can serve such purposes as:

☞ Having the means to join your friends when they go out to a movie, concert, sports event or any outside activity that requires money.

☞ Being able to make your own choices about how you will spend it. A liberating experience for some.

☞ Being able to afford at least some of the little things and big things of life, such as a new pair of jeans or a four-speaker stereo set.

☞ A sense of security or safety. Many people feel a bit more at ease and venturesome when they have a full wallet.

No one is pleased about the idea of an empty wallet. Aside from the sinking or hollow feeling that empty pockets sometimes brings, a lack of money can be a pretty sour and negative experience—especially when there is something you really want (or want to do). Clearly, life can be brighter and you can see more, do more and perhaps enjoy more if you have enough money. In the chapters that follow, this book will discuss how you can get the money you need, increase your supply, make it multiply, and how to spend it effectively and sensibly.

2

Where Does Your Money Come From?

At one time or another, probably everyone has day-dreamed about having an unlimited supply of money —perhaps from a hidden gold mine or from a rich and eccentric uncle who grows money trees. However, by now, you have probably discovered that the money you need or want generally comes to you from one of the following sources.

☞ An allowance

☞ Money that you earn at a job

☞ Gift and windfall money

☞ Borrowed money

And you have no doubt noticed that the money you receive from these sources may change in amount over time. At first, you will probably obtain most of your financing from parents or relatives in the form of an allowance (and it usually starts small). But as you get older and more self-reliant and independent, money that you earn may replace some or all of your allowance. If borrowed money represents a big portion of your weekly finances, you could be in trouble. Gifts in the form of money can be a nice addition to your income, although if it's a sizeable sum parents tend to take control of the funds. In this chapter, we will take a look at your major money sources, how they change, and what this all means for you.

The Allowance System

Your first steady source of money will most probably be an allowance given to you by your parents or a relative. Some interesting facts about allowances are:

☞ Your parents generally decide when to give you money and how much. In effect, they control the source. Now this can be to your advantage if they are generous and indulgent—ready to support your every need. However, this may not be such a good arrangement if they are very conservative and tight about supplying you with funds. And worse yet, you may discover that one of the undesirable features of your allowance is that your parents use it as a reward and punishment device (guess what may happen when they get upset about some of your behavior).

☞ Your allowance may be arranged as a set weekly amount or supplied on a demand basis—when you need money you ask for it. If you are given a fixed weekly amount, be sure that it is enough. Do some simple calculations with your parents so that everyone knows how much is needed and just exactly what items the allowance is supposed to cover.

☞ If it's a flexible "on demand" basis, the system certainly favors you unless you ask for too much too often and your parents get the idea that you are too demanding.

If your parents' responses turn a bit sticky or resistant, perhaps you should talk to them about establishing a fixed weekly allowance.

☞ The big question is "how much allowance is enough?" There aren't any easy answers—especially when you discover that your money needs just naturally increase each year. If you are uncertain about what's a reasonable sum, ask your friends what kind of an allowance they receive. Do a bit of investigating and then sit down with your parents and tell them what you found out. Another approach is to make a list of your weekly needs—lunch money, transportation, snack money, and then add an amount for entertainment. What's important is that you get involved in the process of establishing a reasonable allowance for you. It's a good way to start taking charge of your expenses, and who knows, it may lead to your being given a nice healthy allowance.

☞ Some allowances are directly related to the performance of some chores on a regular basis. Washing dishes, doing the gardening, running errands, washing windows and helping with the laundry are just a few of the tasks that may be assigned to you. In essence, you are working for your money. As the economists would say you are receiving income (money) for services performed (your chores). For many families this is considered a sensible and practical way to approach the financial needs of younger family members. And it certainly can be a sound solution unless . . . you have trouble completing the chores. Maybe you were given too many assignments at school or a heavy chore load. Whatever the problem, when things don't get done it can threaten your allowance and cause family tension.

☞ Parents may need to be educated about special arrangements. Many young people have worked out a special system of borrowing ahead or obtaining "advances." These are additional sums given on demand and paid back later or deducted from future allowances. With this system you can obtain money for those very special occasions or special purchases such as a much wanted pair of second-hand skis or a Sunfish sailboat offered at a fraction of the store price.

Money That You Earn

Lots of people have discovered that earning money from a part-time job can be rewarding both financially and personally. Consider what happens when you do some work for pay.

☞ You immediately add to your spendable weekly income. If you also get an allowance, the extra money from your job gives you more to spend. Unless, of course, your parents decide to reduce your allowance or, perish the thought, cease giving you one.

☞ You can begin to save for something special. Maybe it's a ten-speed bicycle, a new stereo set or a second-hand car. By earning your own money you won't have to wait twenty years until you have accumulated enough gift money to afford that special something.

☞ With money that you earn you can usually go more places and do more things—especially now when the price of entertainment (and everything else) seems to increase virtually overnight.

☞ And, naturally, by earning your own money you are showing yourself and others that you can take responsibility for your own needs. Your own money also allows you to be less dependent on the generosity of your parents.

Quite possibly, what you earn at some outside job may be sufficient to meet all of your money needs. Or perhaps what you earn only takes care of some of your weekly expenses. What you will probably notice as you begin to generate your own income are two great mysteries of the modern world.

☞ Generally, the more money you have, the more you will spend.

☞ The older you get, the more money you require just to get through the week.

Scientists and many parents have carefully investigated these phenomena and have been unable to discover the causes.

Just how you can get started earning your own money is described in detail in Chapter 5. Once you start, it's quite likely that you will be tempted to neglect your studies in little ways. Try not to let this happen. One way to avoid this potential problem is to limit the number of hours that you work. You have an entire lifetime of work ahead of you, so why not start slow and enjoy your studies and your friends.

Gift and Windfall Money

Just about everyone knows about gift money—it's cash money that you get at your birthday, Christmas or some other special occasion. Sometimes you can plan on receiving it. For example, your grandparents in Florida always send you ten dollars on your birthday or your Uncle Jim always sends you cash at Christmas. While it's a pretty predictable source of income, you can never be quite certain that it will arrive any given year. And, unfortunately, it's the kind of money you can't really spend until you get it.

Now the Merriam-Webster Dictionary defines a windfall as "an unexpected sudden gift, gain or advantage." Maybe you have won the church raffle or the local lottery—or perhaps you found a five dollar bill on the street. Whatever the source, it's random, unpredictable cash that finds its way into your hands. While windfall money is certainly income, you can't really plan on it or use it until you have it.

Fortunately, one of the pleasurable facts about windfall or gift money is that it can be a large sum.

Borrowed Money

A fourth source of money, and sometimes a most welcome one, is borrowed money. Borrowing is probably the most popular means of obtaining money on short notice, especially when you are away from home. If your credit is good (that means the one you are trying to borrow from believes that you will return the money) borrowed money is a ready and convenient source.

There is one notable thing about borrowed money that you shouldn't forget. It's on loan to you and you are expected to return it. To borrow is to receive with the intention of returning. It helps to establish, at the time you borrow, a repayment date, and then do your best to repay promptly.

When you suddenly have the urge or need to borrow, for whatever the reason, here is some advice you may want to think about.

☞ Only borrow the amount you think you will need.

☞ Try not to borrow a sum so large that will strip you of your next few weekly allowances to pay it back. Keep your borrowing at the simple level.

☞ If you absolutely must have a fairly sizeable sum of money, for whatever reason, consider discussing a loan arrangement with your parents first. Perhaps you can pay it out over a longer period, work it off or make some other special arrangements.

☞ If you can, avoid the habit of borrowing often or from many sources. One good way to limit your borrowing, particularly from friends or relatives, is to be more careful of your money needs. More about this later.

3

Where Does Your Money Go?

While some of the best things in life are still free, you may find it's not always that easy when you're hungry for a slice of pizza or want to see the latest movie. Unfortunately, the pizza parlor owner and the woman at the movie ticket booth still expect cash. And, since many of your future encounters for goods and services will be on a cash transaction basis, you had best be prepared to pay your own way—or have someone with you who can.

If you have taken any interest at all in the ebb and flow of your money over the past year or two, you have probably noticed that:

☞ Your money goes too quickly. It can literally disappear right before your very eyes.

☞ A lot of your money is spent on simple, everyday basics.

☞ Having a good time with friends gets more and more expensive.

How Quickly It Goes

Unless you are very lucky or very rich, you have probably experienced that sinking feeling in the pit of your stomach when you realized that you didn't have enough money for transportation home, to buy a hamburger, purchase a new record or take someone for ice cream after the movie. Don't think you are the only one suddenly struck poor—it happens to just about everyone. It will help you if you keep in mind three major facts of life about your money.

FACT 1

Your money needs will increase! What was enough last year won't be enough this year and most certainly won't be enough next year.

FACT 2

The price of almost everything you like and enjoy will increase—faster it seems than the things you don't like. Inflation can reduce the value of your money. Remember what a slice of pizza and a Coca Cola cost two years ago? Things don't normally get less expensive.

FACT 3

You can expect to engage in some money and allowance bargaining with your parents just about every year (unless you are working and supporting yourself completely). It makes good sense to discuss your money needs with your parents. They may not have noticed that your particular wants and basic everyday needs are changing.

Where Your Money Goes

While it's no secret that everybody spends their money differently, there are some general patterns to most people's expenditures. To some extent, your money-spending habits will be pretty much influenced by such factors as:

☞ your age

☞ your interests

☞ your family's financial status

☞ whether you have a job

☞   where you live

☞   your life style

☞   what your friends are doing

The money requirements of young people increase sharply when they start going out. A seventeen-year-old young man with his own car and a girlfriend needs a pretty full wallet to get through a week—certainly more than a thirteen-year-old who prefers a baseball game or a video game contest. If you happen to be a girl in the eighth grade, your needs and wants are probably a lot more basic and less expensive than the high school girl in a competition marching band. Even if your name is Orphan Annie and you have Daddy Warbucks for a father, you will still have to worry about money.

Assuming that you are like most young people, you can expect that most of your money will be spent on the following:

Your Everyday Needs

Simple everyday items generally take the biggest bite out of your weekly money supply. Traveling to and from school, lunch at school, snacks after school (or all day)—perhaps a pack of cigarettes—this is where it goes. To be more specific, you can expect, whether you like it or not, to spend a pretty sizeable fortune over the next few years on the following items:

☞ Transportation

☞ Lunches, snacks, candy

☞ Music records, tapes, books

☞ Clothing and accessories

☞ Hobby materials, sporting goods

☞ Cosmetics, toiletries

☞ School supplies

☞ Gifts for relatives and friends

Nothing extravagant or unusual about the list—just everyday items. And, as you have probably guessed, the list of everyday necessities will grow right along with you.

Your Social Life

Since few people live like hermits in caves, you can expect to spend a good bit of your life with friends and relatives. And when people get together they generally like to go places and do things—most of which involves spending money for entertainment and food. What was once all very simple begins to get more complicated and expensive. There was a time when your parents took you out and paid for everything. Then you discovered science fiction movies, horror films, the local electronic game center—and you found that your parents lost their enthusiasm. So you had to start using your own money—no more free rides.

Once you get to the world of music, discos, roller rinks and sporting events, the generation gap widens, and you find that your parents aren't prepared to "treat you" to everything. And, you've noticed that the good times are becoming very expensive—maybe pushing your allowance to the limit.

The cost of transportation, admission to the event, snack, meal, tip and maybe parking fees can put a big dent in anybody's weekly budget. And, unless you are planning to get married at fourteen to avoid the costs of going out, be prepared to spend more and more as you get older and go out more.

Young women are no longer immune from the plague of escalating finances once they start going out. More girls are paying their own way now. Also, your clothing, cosmetics and jewelry needs will probably expand as you become more aware of how to look your best. Moreover, as your interest in the opposite sex grows (and it probably will as you do) you can expect to find yourself going to events with your girlfriends—just to meet some attractive, interesting young men. Dances, rock concerts, sailing, swimming, skiing—they are all great fun and give you an opportunity to meet new friends. And most of it costs money. One thing for sure—your old allowance or budget just won't do once you get in the swing of things.

Those Special Things

In addition to the monies you will require for everyday needs and entertaining, you can expect that a fairly large chunk of your money will be spent on those special things. For many it will be musical equipment, maybe a guitar, a motorbike, skis, ten-speed bicycle, a trip to Washington, D.C. in the spring with the school class, or a week's survival course at Outward Bound. Whatever the special things are in your life, they have some common characteristics.

☞ Those special items are much more costly than your everyday or weekly budget expenditures.

☞ Getting them will probably involve some special effort, planning, and negotiations with your parents or others.

☞ You may have to start a special savings program, do some extra chores at home, or find a part-time job.

☞ If you are very enterprising, you may engage in some barter or trading with others in order to raise all or some of the money needed for these special things.

Maybe you have been lucky so far and your parents have willingly provided the money for the special things you have wanted. Chances are that there will come a day when you will hear those very unpopular words, "No, I'm sorry, we just don't have the money for that," or maybe the statement will be, "If we give you the money for the (whatever it is) we will deduct it from your weekly allowance—so much each week."

Whatever the words are, the meaning is pretty much the same. You have just run out of readily available funds.

Saving Some of Your Money

When your weekly allowance will hardly take you from Monday through Friday (never mind the weekend), the idea of putting some of it into savings borders on the insane. However, if you do put some away, it will be there when you want those special things that you can't possibly manage to pay for out of your regular weekly allowance or budget.

It's Your Money

One of the important points to remember about your money is that it *is* yours—to be spent the way you want on the things you want. If you like ice cream or pizza and you have the money to buy them—do it. Somewhere, someone in your life may not appreciate the way you spend your money. Their words may go something like this:

> "What are you doing with all your money—spending it on junk?"

> "How can you waste your money on that trash?"

> "All you do is throw away your money on that worthless stuff (movies, music, etc.)."

Keep in mind that everyone is conditioned differently—some grow up with what seems to be very strange ideas about how money should be spent and for what purposes. Their ideas and notions about money don't have to be yours. Sure, you will have to allocate some of your money for essentials, such as transportation and lunches, but a good bit of your money should be for you to spend on what pleases you. If you don't learn to spend some of it on things you like and enjoy (and you deserve to have some enjoyment with it) then you may have trouble with money later on in your life. So respect it, but spend it the way you want, for what you want. Nobody can live your life for you so don't look to others to tell you how to spend your money.

4

How to Take Charge of Your Money

Given their choices, most people, of all ages, would probably prefer a nice simple life without any concern or worry about money. Ideally, it would be great if you could just turn on a water faucet and bills poured out, or you had a money tree in your back yard and you just went out and picked some whenever there was a need. While it's great to dream, real life is a good bit different and you have to pay careful attention to your sources of income. And, since some people don't watch their money very carefully, neglect can cause problems.

There are about four basic money conditions in this world. They are as follows:

1. You have all the money you want whenever you need it. (Wouldn't that be great!)

2. You have enough for your needs and wants. Your weekly income is sufficient but you have to be careful and sensible.

3. Your money income is usually not quite enough. It's touch and go. You have good weeks when there is enough but there are far too many weeks when you run out too quickly or just can't make it through without minor assistance or giving up something.

4. Money and you are virtually strangers. You suffer from a chronic shortage that cuts into your essentials and doesn't afford you the funds to enjoy even some of the simple, inexpensive pleasures of life.

If you classify yourself in either the first or second category above—you probably don't have much in the way of money problems. And, if by some stroke of fortune you have so much money that you can't figure out how to spend it all—ask your friends to help you. That should prove interesting!

If you fit into one of the last two conditions above,

particularly the last one, you could probably benefit from some of the suggestions and simple exercises that are set forth in this chapter. Unfortunately, it's never too early to begin to take charge of and be responsible for your money. Not many people really enjoy taking care of their money in a sensible manner. Like so many other things in life they end up doing it because nobody else wants to—and if they don't they know they are in for trouble.

A Dollar Short

There is an old saying that some people have turned into a way of life: "I'm always either a day late or a dollar short." It describes a way of living that isn't much fun and usually gets worse as the person gets older—particularly the part about lack of money. Too often people find themselves broke, angry, discouraged and/or embarassed because they have:

☞ spent what they had too quickly

☞ spent what they had recklessly or extravagantly

☞ failed to ask for enough or to bring enough with them

☞ been unwilling to or don't know how to supplement an allowance that just won't cover their needs and wants (getting a part-time job or doing special chores).

These disappointing situations often occur because a person doesn't know about the simple ways that can keep one from being a dollar short all the time. A lot of the discomfort of empty pockets can be eliminated if the sufferer just puts into practice these simple steps:

☞ Monitor your money needs, review your expenses, list what's essential and what isn't.

☞ Communicate your needs. Tell your parents about your problems, your cash needs and what you have discovered when you reviewed your cash situation.

☞ Contribute to your needs. Most young people are strong enough, capable enough and have time enough to earn some money to eliminate their state of poverty.

☞ Spend your money more carefully. Teach yourself to be more sensible and conservative about spending—at least until your fortunes change and you get more to spend. Try not to buy things on a whim, be more deliberate in your purchase behavior.

☞ If you are one who borrows a lot, see if you can limit the amount of debt you incur each week. If you can learn to hold back every so often and not borrow, you won't have as much to pay back the following week.

If you find that no matter what you do, you still suffer from the common problems associated with weekly poverty, perhaps you could benefit from some simple money planning exercises—also known as budgeting. Don't let the word "budgeting" drive you away. It's nothing complicated or overwhelming. It's merely the application of some common sense to your way of handling money. The overall goal of any money planning is to help you get more enjoyment and satisfaction in your life as a result of more sensible and practical personal money management. With twenty minutes or one-half hour of effort you can be well on your way to a much more relaxed and less frantic way of taking care of your money needs. Instead of postponing or skipping over the next section, try reading about budgeting with an open mind. Sooner or later you will probably have to concern yourself with some money management activities. Why not enjoy a sneak preview—and then laugh at yourself when you realize how simple it all is!

How to Establish a Money Plan

Before we get into the details and specifics, let's look at some simple requirements that a money plan should fulfill. The plan:

☞ Should not be complicated or difficult to develop.

☞ Should fit your particular needs and problems.

☞ Should be workable—it's no good if you can't actually put it into practice.

☞ Should bring you some relief, some positive re-sults.

Keep in mind that once you have put together your simple money plan or budget program you have to put it to work—you have to stick to your suggestions. You have to take the steps to bring about change. And if you just don't want all the hassle and responsibility of fol-lowing the plan you develop—you have found out something about yourself, you just aren't willing to take some steps to get rid of your money problems.

Now, on to the easy-to-do steps needed to work up a budget or money plan.

☞ Keep a simple record (daily if possible) of just what you do with your money in the course of a week. List on a sheet of paper how much you spend for transportation, food, snacks, movies, hobby materials, cosmetics, club dues, school events, gifts, dates, gas. Whatever you spend be sure to record it. It certainly shouldn't take you more than a few minutes a day. Now do this for a couple of weeks—or if you really find it kind of interesting, try to record three weeks of expen-ditures. In addition to your expenditures, be sure to keep a record of all monies you are given or earn during these weeks. This is your income, the amount you had available to spend during this time. Finally, make a note of what amount of money you had left at the end of each week. Your record for a particular week might look like this:

Weekly Expenses Item	Amount	Weekly Income Received Amount	What's Left
Lunches	$ 5.00	$10.00	
Snacks	4.00	3.00	
Movie	3.50	5.00	
Transportation	3.00	5.00	
Club Dues	1.00		
Batteries	1.50		
School Supplies	1.50		
Magazines	2.75		
	$22.25	$23.00	$.75

The purpose of this record is to give you a picture of just where your money goes and how much you have left at the end of each week. Now if you borrow some money to get through the week—don't put that in your income column because it isn't really income —you have to repay it. In the example list above, if the last five dollars had been borrowed, your weekly record would read as follows:

Expenses	Income	What's Left
$22.25	$18.00	− $4.25

You spent four dollars and twenty-five cents more than you had received as income from your parents, work or gift money.

Once you have a picture of what you do with your money you can create a simple summary of your financial status.

☞ Prepare a simple money summary chart based upon the records you kept over the past few weeks. Just divide a sheet of paper into three sections and list the following:

a) What money you generally or typically get each week and from what sources.

b) The amount of money you spend each week on essential items—those which are pretty necessary. List down the essential items and what amount you typically spend each week.

c) The amount of money you generally spend on nonessential items such as candy, soft drinks, video games, lottery tickets, movies, stereo tapes, dating, magazines and other things.

It would be great if after all your expenditures, you still have some money left over to put away into savings or to set aside for something special. But let's take a look at how a typical summary chart might appear:

Money I Usually Get in a Typical Week

Source	Amount
Allowance	$10.00
Part-time job	10.00
Special chores	3.00
Total Weekly Income	$23.00

Essential Expenses (Necessary Weekly Items)

Item	Amount
School lunches	$5.00
Bus fare	3.00
Club dues	1.00
Batteries	1.50
School supplies	1.50
Total Essential Expenses	$12.00

Nonessential or Optional Purchases

Item	Amount
Snacks	$4.00
Movie	3.50
Magazines	2.75
Total Nonessential	$10.25

Naturally, your nonessential items can include a lot of things that you buy only occasionally or would like to buy when you have extra money. The summary chart shows you a few important facts:

☞ There is only seventy-five cents left over for saving or for special needs or emergency funds.

☞ A very large proportion of the weekly expenditures is for nonessential items.

$\dfrac{\$10.25}{\$23.00}$ 45% for   nonessential items

If this person suddenly ran into tough times when there was no part-time work (ten dollars income weekly) he or she could still survive and be able to take care of the essential expenses. Now let's assume that this person is concerned about buying a new Walkman stereo portable radio and wants to start saving for it. What can be done? Well, the person can ask for a larger allowance, do more part-time work or cut down on some of the nonessential expenses such as snacks and magazines. He or she might spend only three dollars a week on snacks and only a dollar on magazines. In that way, two dollars and seventy five-cents can be saved each week.

By now, you have probably figured out that, if you develop a simple chart of your income and expenses, you can see more clearly what is happening to your money and the areas where you can consider or create changes. Most importantly, if you discover that your weekly expenses are consistently equal to or greater than your weekly income, you should make some effort to either increase your income or reduce your weekly expenses or perhaps do both. In this chapter we are focusing on your expense items while chapter 12 discusses ways of increasing your income.

There are some decisions involved in reviewing what you have been doing with your money and how to make it all work more effectively. First, there is the definition of an "essential" or necessary expense. For many young people anything they want or like is a "necessary" expense. That's the self-indulgent approach and unless you are loaded with money, you can't just go around buying anything you want, because the funds will quickly run out. So let's say that lunches, transportation, school supplies, club dues or special lessons fees are all essential expenditures. An extra hamburger in the middle of the afternoon, five video games at an arcade, a lottery ticket, two candy bars, or a pack of cigarettes are not essential to your health, schooling or well-being. Certainly you deserve some fun in life, but none of these are necessary. Often, the way to get your money into more manageable shape is to determine which group of nonessential pleasures you are willing to give up or reduce. Maybe you need more money for dating—think about cutting down on those random midafternoon snacks—or if you are always, always hungry, bring some extra food from home. Let's face it, you can't have everything you want, and you have to learn a bit of restraint in order to get some of the most important things.

Another issue you need to look at is unexpected expenses that suddenly occur. Do you want to put away or save a little money each week for these surprise needs? If you decide you are happy just making your income equal expenses each week that's fine. You may just have to accept the fact that unexpected expenses will always make a mess of your weekly money plans. But it's usually easier to set aside some money in advance.

Now that you have read all of this and done the exercises, maybe you still aren't sure what to do about it. The first objective was to get you to look at how you handle money. The second objective is to suggest that you make up a weekly budget plan (how you feel you should spend your money) so that you get the most benefit from your income. Here is one possible way to set up a plan that permits some saving as well as daily expenditures that aren't too depriving.

BUDGET PLAN

Weekly Income		$23.00
Weekly Expenses		
School lunches	$ 5.00	
Bus fare	3.00	
Club dues	1.00	
School supplies	3.00	
Snacks	3.00	
Movie	3.50	
Magazines	1.00	
Total Expenses	$19.50	
Savings/Emergency Money		$ 3.50
Total Expenses and Saving		$23.00

It doesn't do any harm to enlist your parent's help in this whole effort since it will:

☞ Demonstrate to them that you are interested in being responsible about your money.

☞ Give them an opportunity to guide you and help you.

☞ Provide you with an opportunity to ask for a little additional money if they are receptive.

There is one aspect of budgeting that you should keep firmly in mind. Once you establish a budget plan, you should try to stick to it—even if it hurts or makes you angry. It's not always fun and you will certainly have plenty of temptations, but it is good training for taking charge of your life.

And don't forget, it's a sensible idea to develop a new budget plan at least once a year, because your money needs will probably change in some way each year—and maybe your income won't keep up with your needs.

Putting a Little Money Aside

For some people, saving is natural and easy; but for most young people, trying to put aside a dollar or a few dollars each week is a very difficult, if not impossible, task. To ask someone to consider putting a little money aside each week may seem impractical when their money doesn't even seem to stretch to the end of the week. But with a bit of budget planning it often can be done. There are three sound reasons for making an effort to save a little each week.

1. The time will come when you will have a chance to buy, see or visit something very important to you—but you won't have any extra money—and there will be no readily available source of extra money.

2. The money you save will add up and then you will have an opportunity to buy something special for yourself.

3. The money will be there for an unexpected emergency, from replacing a window you broke to repairing your car or bicycle.

Of course, learning how to save when you are young makes it that much easier when you get older. Saving can be habit forming. Remember, if you do decide to save each week—either open a savings account or give it to your parents to hold. If you just keep it handy or carry it in your pocket, you might lose it or, worse, you might be tempted to spend it every week because it's immediately available.

If you still can't work your budget plan and save any money, get creative. Ask your parents to help you to work out ways to earn some extra money—to be set aside for saving and special occasions. Look around your home for any special chores your parents don't like that you could volunteer to do for pay to go directly into savings. If not at home, how about in the neighborhood—most people would welcome paying a small amount to have someone else do some bothersome chores.

Getting Advice

All through this chapter it has been suggested that you seek your parents' advice. They probably would welcome all your concern and interest. Maybe an older brother or sister could also be of assistance. It's best, though, to stay clear of friends or relatives who have a lot of trouble managing their own money. They probably won't be too sensible a source of guidance.

If you feel that your parents or other relatives won't be helpful, ask around at school to determine what teacher or counselor can help you with simple budget planning. Guidance counselors or home economics teachers may be good sources. Don't be afraid to ask. You are to be congratulated for your wisdom, not laughed at because you are interested in managing your money well.

5

How to Earn Your Own Money

Contrary to what you may think, there really are dozens, if not hundreds, of ways to earn money. And they don't involve sweat shop conditions, long hours, or unhealthy or illegal activities. Maybe you've decided that it's time to consider a job or a source of income other than your family. Whatever the motivation, whether prompted by:

☞ An allowance that just doesn't make it from one end of the week to the next

☞ The desire for something big and special (stereo set, electric guitar, your own car)

☞ Too many hassles over money; too many debts, too many events missed just because of empty pockets

☞ The realization that it's probably not a bad idea to start carrying your own weight and taking more responsibility for your own financial needs

rest assured, there are plenty of opportunities out there. And these opportunities don't involve petty theft or working for a local dope dealer. The prospects of locating work that will produce income needn't frighten you or leave you feeling hopelessly inadequate or confused. Remember, millions of young people your age have successfully found opportunities to generate their own income. Moreover, recent national statistics indicate that at least one-half of all young adults in the fourteen to nineteen age category have some kind of job outside the home.

Your chances of successfully landing a job will probably be enhanced if you do a little advance planning and follow some simple job-hunting suggestions. That's what this chapter is all about.

Earning Money at Home

A little practice at home and in your local neighborhood can help you in your efforts to earn your own money. Most young people start by doing a few home chores for small sums of money. The key is to be alert to the opportunities that exist right in your own household—or close by. Pay attention to those domestic chores that your parents find bothersome. Look for projects that you feel uniquely capable of handling. Some examples of such opportunities might be:

☞ Mowing the lawn (yours or others') and yard work

☞ Baby-sitting

☞ Dog-walking, pet-sitting

☞ Washing, polishing cars

☞ Washing the pots and pans or dishes (ugh)

☞ Washing windows, washing and waxing floors, vacuum cleaning

☞ Chopping wood

☞ Shoveling snow

☞ Running special errands

☞ Painting the house, fences, garage

Just listen to what people gripe about and keep in mind that there may be income-producing opportunities in those grumbles.

Getting a Part-Time Job

CONSIDER YOUR TIME SCHEDULE

When you decide to look for something more substantial outside of your home (or local neighborhood), it's a good idea to examine your daily and weekly schedule to determine just what time you have available for work. You may find that:

☞ You have a busy school schedule until late every weekday.

☞ You have special school-related commitments on three afternoons.

☞ You have certain chores at home that prevent you from working early in the evenings (helping with meals, taking care of younger brothers or sisters).

☞ Your Saturdays are spent at a vacation house, football practice or shopping.

☞ Your Sundays are devoted to religion, chores, or visiting relatives.

The important thing is to look over your use of time and your weekly schedule to find out when you

are most available. You may find that you can only
work:

☞   Afternoons between 2–6 P.M.

☞   Saturdays only

☞   Weekends only

☞   Two or three evenings a week

To a greater or lesser extent your available time
will have a lot to do with the kind of part-time job
opportunities you investigate. It won't help to look for
work as a waitress if you can't work during the high-
traffic meal hours. If you can only work Saturday and
Sunday mornings its pretty doubtful that you will get
a job as an usher in a theater.

There are two other factors you should also examine before you start your part-time search:

☞   How well are you doing with your school work?
    Will a part-time job cut into your study efforts?

☞   How much weekly income do you want?

If you only need a few extra dollars a week, it isn't
wise to take on a job that will commit you to fifteen or
twenty hours of work. It's better to try for jobs with
limited or very flexible hours. Many young adults tend
to take on a more extensive work schedule than they
need, and their school work suffers along with their

social life and their sense of humor. Remember, you have all the rest of your life to work and, unless you are absolutely driven to be financially productive every spare moment, start slowly with a limited schedule. And if you are working primarily to save for something special, try to stretch out your saving period—frantic enforced savings can put extra strain on you and put your life out of balance.

WHAT KIND OF WORK?

There are generally two approaches to this issue:

☞ Any kind that I can get or any place that will have me,

☞ Some kind of work that's meaningful, enjoyable or fits my temperament, life interests or future plans.

Alas, too many job seekers fall into the first category—and maybe that's just the way things are in life. It's pretty difficult to screen job opportunities and deliberate on the value, merits and potential fit of a position, if you don't have any burning special interests, established goals—or if you are really pressed for money. Sometimes getting a part-time job is as simple as applying for work at a local McDonalds, where your closest friend is working, or at the discount drug store where your brother once worked.

Sad to say, most part-time jobs are "just jobs"—nothing magical, stimulating or glorious. But they will provide you with your own money, a sense of independence, and a chance to learn how to function in a work-for-pay situation. It's all part of getting some experience.

Psychologists have long maintained that people work better if they have a vital interest in what they do and derive a lot of satisfaction from their efforts. This certainly is reason enough to pause and take a bit of time to look over what your interests are and the kinds of activities you enjoy. Just maybe there is a job opportunity that coincides with your area of interest. Some examples might be:

Area of Interest	*Where To Look*
Tinkering with cars/engines	Local garage/service station
Reading	Library, bookstore
Acting/theater	Usher, stagehand
Music	Music store, band, music hall
Golf	Country club, sporting goods store

FINDING PART-TIME WORK

If you are pretty sure about the kind of work that interests you, your task is a bit easier than those who have no specific job in mind. For the person who is interested in auto mechanics and wants a job at a gas station or garage, the approach might be:

☞ Make a list of all the gas stations and garages in the community or neighborhood,

☞ Visit them in person and ask the manager about part-time openings. It's best not to rely on the word of anyone except the station or garage manager. He is the only one who knows what size staff he needs—and who he might be planning to replace,

☞ Telephone the station managers if your list is lengthy. You may save a lot of travel time and effort by initially screening the stations and garages by telephone.

☞ Inquire at your school guidance office. At most schools, one of the staff handles part-time job requests from local businesses.

☞ Ask your friends, relatives and neighbors if they know of any part-time openings. Don't be afraid to ask them to keep your needs in mind. It's perfectly acceptable to enlist others in your job search. Remember, job seeking requires some extra effort and sometimes it can be a bit discouraging. If you keep at it, you'll probably land the job you want.

This approach can work for just about any job search where you know the kind of work that interests you. But what do you do if you have no special interests or don't feel particularly qualified for any special kind of work activity? Don't despair—there is plenty that you can do to get yourself a part-time job. Before you start, have it clear in your mind just what hours you want to work. Many job opportunities will probably be eliminated right at the start because the hours will conflict with your school or personal/family schedule. After you have done some talking with friends, parents, and relatives about jobs in general and where you might fit in—your job search might be easier if you keep in mind the following suggestions:

☞ Check the help wanted ads in your local newspaper including the shopper circulars and papers that may be delivered to your home free.

☞ Read the bulletin board notices at your supermarket, bowling alley—any place where public notices are posted.

☞ Watch for "help wanted" signs in the front window of businesses.

☞ Be sure to inquire at your school guidance office, placement counselor or local city/state employment office.

☞ Ask your friends—especially those who have part-time jobs—if they know of any opportunities.

APPLYING FOR THE JOB

Once you have uncovered a part-time job opportunity, you will most likely be required to personally meet with the manager or owner. Here are some hints and tips that can assist you.

☞ If you have a set appointment get there on time.

☞ Be sure to have your Social Security card, working papers, or birth certificate with you. Most businesses need this basic information for their tax and accounting records.

☞ Your clothes and personal grooming are important. You will help your chances if you dress neatly and cleanly—a pair of dirty jeans, beat-up shoes, and a well-traveled tee-shirt won't help you much at an interview at McDonald's or the local library.

☞ Describe your time schedule, available hours and capabilities. This can prevent confusion or misunderstanding about the job hours. If there is conflict, maybe a flexible schedule can be worked out.

☞ Do ask about the hourly pay (and tipping practices if included in the compensation). Also ask about lunch/dinner breaks if the job involves long hours. Don't hesitate to ask about how you should dress for work. Some places will have uniforms and others may be largely indifferent to a dress code, but it is best to ask.

☞ Do ask how often you will be paid (weekly, every two weeks) and whether you will be paid cash or by check.

☞ If you are applying for summer work or a seasonal job, be sure to apply well in advance. They often have waiting lists.

☞ Finally, if you feel a bit nervous or uncertain about yourself when you go for the interview, try to keep in mind that your reactions are pretty natural and the person evaluating you understands your desire to make a good impression. If you don't get the job, try not to be discouraged. There's a part-time job waiting for you and you will find it if you keep looking.

Try not to be too concerned about your talents or ability to do the work required. Most part-time jobs—even the more complicated ones—can be mastered in a few days or a week. You may not know all of the details, but in short time your performance will be quite acceptable.

Some Unusual Job Opportunities

Maybe you aren't exactly sure what kind of part-time work you would like, but you know you would be happier if you stayed away from the everyday jobs such as store clerk, waitress, delivery boy, car washer, or movie usher. With a little resourcefulness, courage and creativity you can find some challenging, interesting, maybe even exciting part-time jobs. For example:

☞ If you like animals or are interested in becoming a nurse or doctor—how about looking for a job at a veterinarian's office or an animal hospital or in a people's hospital, lab or clinic.

☞ If you enjoy photography, apply for work at the commercial photography studios, advertising agencies or local television stations. (Don't forget the cable TV company.)

☞ If you are hooked on a musical instrument why not apply for work with a fledgling music group, musical instrument store (good for contacts) or at any one of the local radio stations. Many stations have some pretty talented people who might further your career. Concert and recital halls also employ part-time help.

☞ For those who are interested in health and beauty aids there are opportunities at the local health food stores, skin care studios, beauty salons, health clubs, reducing spas or cosmetic counters.

☞ If you are interested in the crafts such as pottery, woodworking, painting, don't overlook local cabinetry shops, pottery studios, frame shops, commercial design or artist studios, interior design firms or printshops.

☞ If you think you would be good at clerical or administrative tasks, do look into museums, United Way chapters, Red Cross, church administrative offices, Boys Clubs, YMCA, YWCA chapters.

☞ If you are interested in travel you might contact local travel agencies, transportation firms (bus, train, airline) or the travel department of major companies. If your desire for travel is overwhelming, you can always join the Navy or Army Reserve—they're pretty good about sending you to remote corners of the world.

Once you have pretty well decided that you want something different in the way of a part-time job, gaining knowledge about what's around is important.

☞ Canvass your local area. See what kinds of businesses and services there are.

☞ Visit your local Chamber of Commerce and ask for a list of local firms.

☞ Check the Yellow Pages—just about every business operating in your area will be listed. You will be surprised at the many unusual ones. Quite probably some of them might offer challenging opportunities.

However you approach your part-time job search, the more exposure to different kinds of jobs, the better your chances of selecting an opportunity that fits who you are and what you feel comfortable doing for wages.

6

Where to Keep Your Money

Now that you find yourself with some surplus money
—that's money that you don't need immediately—you
may suddenly discover that you need someplace to
keep it safe. There are many solutions to this problem
and over time you may try them all. Perhaps you have
already tried some of the simplest methods such as:

☞ Under your mattress

☞ In your bottom dresser drawer

☞ Rolled up in one of your socks

☞ Hidden in a stuffed doll or pillow

One great advantage of these hiding places is their accessibility. The money is right at your fingertips. However, once your money begins to build up and the sum gets sizeable you might consider what would happen if you have a curious dog who finds stuffed dolls a gourmet delicacy or a compulsive mother who cleans socks every week without looking to see what might be inside them. In other words, as your money increases so does the element of risk.

There are a number of additional ways to safeguard your money. The principal ones are:

☞ Give it to your parents or other relative

☞ Put it in a bank

☞ Invest it

Many people have taken advantage of all of the above methods. For many, they are progressive stages that become important as your money grows. Some of the key features and facts about each method are described below.

Letting Your Parents Hold Your Money

One way that many parents help their children is by guiding them with their earliest money transactions. In addition to providing an allowance or ready supply of money, parents often safeguard their children's surplus money until the children need it. Parents can be a great help if you receive money in the form of a personal check as they can have it cashed. Since some banks refuse to cash personal checks unless you are a customer, it's nice to have helpful parents.

There are some pretty sound benefits to having your parents or other family member act as banker. These include:

☞ Your money is immediately available, usually. If you are considering using it all in the near future, it helps to notify your parents in advance. They may have mingled your money with theirs and they may require a day or two to get extra cash.

☞ You have no need to keep records. Chances are your parents will keep some kind of tally or accounting for you.

☞ You don't have to worry about the red tape and procedures involved if you had kept your money in a bank. Also, your parents are available seven days a week, day and night; most banks don't provide you with such access.

☞ You can readily borrow small or large sums secured (guaranteed) by the money your parents are safekeeping for you. This of course assumes that the amount you wish to borrow is less than the amount your parents are holding.

☞ You don't have to concern yourself with how the money is being cared for. All you really need to know is that it is available and you can add to it or subtract from it when you wish.

Putting Your Money in a Bank

Banks have been around for a long time. They are financial institutions of various kinds that help people of all ages with their money needs and money transactions. They safeguard people's money, lend money, cash checks and provide a whole range of special money services. If you are looking for a safe place to keep your money, you might consider opening a savings account or checking account at a savings bank or commercial bank. These types of banks will accept your money, keep it safe (they even insure it for you) for when you want it and also in a savings account pay you a small sum (called interest) for the use of your money. The amount that a bank will pay you depends on how much money you put in the bank. The interest that a bank will pay you is a percent of the money you deposit. This percent (rate of interest) is fixed by law.

If you open a checking account, you will be given a book of blank checks and you can use these checks to pay for the goods and services that you want. The bank will honor your check and pay to the checkholder the face amount or sum of money written on the check. The following sections tell you about savings accounts and checking accounts, where to go and how to open an account.

A SAVINGS ACCOUNT

Where to go?

You can visit just about any bank and find it willing to provide you with a savings account.

Are there any age requirements?

In most states, banks are prepared to open a savings account for any individual regardless of age. The individual can make his or her own deposits and withdrawals. In a few states a parent or guardian must be a partner in the account (joint savings account). In every state, a parent may open an account for a child of any age—however, dual responsibility for the account is required. This means that both parent and child may deal with the bank.

How does a savings account work?

You may take your money to the bank, fill out a deposit slip, hand the money and slip to a bank teller. He or she will record your deposit and provide you with some form of receipt to verify the receipt of your money. From the day you deposit your money until you withdraw it, the bank promises to:

☞ Keep it safe and ready for your use

☞ Insure it against loss

☞ Pay you a sum of money (interest) for the use of your money

What records or paperwork are involved?

When you ask to open an account you will be given a simple application to fill out. It will contain questions about your name, address, telephone number and an inquiry as to whether you want the account in only your name (no one else can withdraw the money) or a joint account with perhaps one of your parents.

You will probably be given a small passbook with a number stamped on the cover. This book will contain many blank pages and your name, address and signature. The blank pages will be used by the bank teller or clerk to record each of your deposits, withdrawals and the interest money that your deposited money has earned. You will carry the passbook with you to the bank each time you wish to make a deposit or withdrawal.

In some instances, the bank may not give you a passbook. Instead, they will keep a record of your deposit and withdrawals in their computer and each month they will send you a printed statement that shows each of your deposits, withdrawals and interest money earned.

To make a deposit of your money, you merely fill out a simple three- or four-line form called a deposit slip and hand it to the teller with your money (and passbook if the bank issued one). To take your money out of the bank you use the same procedure except you fill out a withdrawal form and hand it to the teller. In this instance the bank gives you the amount of money you requested. You cannot, however, request that they give you more money than the bank is currently holding for you.

How quickly can I get my money?

You can expect to get your money on demand— that is just as quickly as you present a withdrawal slip. You will be given whatever you requested. While banks reserve the right to pay you your money within a certain number of days after you request it, this legal clause is rarely used.

A CHECKING ACCOUNT

Each day millions of people conduct many of their personal financial transactions with checks. They pay their mortgage payment, their car loan and many other bills by check. A check can be considered another form of money. Simply put, it represents money, and when anyone takes a check to a bank to cash it, the bank gives the person cash—just as long as the person writing the check has sufficient money on deposit at the bank. If someone writes you a check for twenty-five dollars but doesn't have that much money in his or her account, the check will be rejected by the bank. (They will "bounce it" and not pay the sum requested because of insufficient funds.)

While it may all seem very confusing, maintaining your own checking account is reasonably uncomplicated. About three-quarters of all United States households have one or more checking accounts. The following is a brief description of the factors involved in opening a checking account and maintaining it.

Who can open a checking account?

Anyone. However, some states require that you must be eighteen or twenty-one years of age before you can have an account of your own. If you are under the legal age, banks will require that a parent or other adult jointly share the responsibility for the account.

Where and how do I apply?

All commercial banks and many savings banks offer personal checking accounts. In order to apply, simply go to the new accounts desk at the bank and ask for an application for a checking account.

Are there different types of checking accounts?

Yes. There are two general categories—the *regular* checking account and the *special* checking account. In most respects these two types are exactly the same except that the regular checking account has a requirement that you keep a minimum amount of money in your account in order to avoid any bank service charges for regular check transactions. If you don't maintain the required minimum, the bank will levy a small monthly charge to process your checks.

A special checking account has no minimum balance requirement. However, the bank charges you a service charge of fifteen to twenty cents for each check that you write. To determine which account might be best for your needs don't hesitate to ask the bank personnel. While there are some additional types of accounts with special, and often complicated, features, unless you are rolling in money the two basic types of accounts should adequately serve your needs.

What are bank service charges?

Since it costs them money to provide financial services, banks pass along some of their costs to their customers, usually in the form of monthly or per check charges. In addition to the above mentioned charges, the bank may also charge you a fee if they execute a "stop payment" of one of your checks (at your request) or if they have to bounce one of your checks when your account has insufficient funds.

How does a checking account work?

In brief, a bank accepts your money—you deposit any amount you wish with them—and agrees to pay out your money to anyone you designate. You merely take one of your checks, fill in the name of the person you want to receive some of your money, write in the amount involved, then sign your name at the bottom of the check and put in the date. By giving this fully completed check to another person you are in essence instructing your bank to give the designated person some of your money. If you want some money for yourself simply make out the check to yourself and take it to the bank.

If the check is properly completed, your bank will pay out some of your money and deduct the same amount from your account. At the end of each month, the bank will send you an accounting (monthly statement), which will list all of the checks you wrote, any deposits (additional funds you placed in your account) and a calculation of how much money you have in your account after all transactions (your balance).

Are there any special conditions or requirements?

Banks are never happy when you write a check for an amount that is larger than the money you have in your account. This is called an overdraft and in most instances the bank will refuse to pay the money to the designated person (unless you have special overdraft privileges).

Banks require you to accurately fill out the check and date it. They may well refuse to cash the check if you have two different amounts written in or you have signed your name differently than you do on your other checks.

Banks have difficulty with checks that have been altered. If you should accidentally write in the wrong amount, do not erase and correct it. Banks request that you use a fresh blank check and start over.

Does checking account money earn interest?

Generally, money that you put in a regular or special checking account does not earn any interest. However, many banks have begun experimenting with new services whereby interest is paid to certain types of checking accounts where substantial minimum balances are maintained. Be sure to inquire about this feature if you are opening a checking account with a sizeable sum of money.

Is it difficult to keep an accurate record of a checking account?

Actually, it's pretty easy, especially if you only write a few checks a month. The bank does most of the work—sending you a checking account statement which describes all your checking transactions, deposits and any bank charges. To determine or verify the amount of money you have left in your account you can consult your written checks (the bank returns them to you each month) and written records to see if they agree with the bank calculations. Once in a while the bank's computers are in error, but most errors are made by the check writer. Since banks have to help customers when there is confusion about a monthly balance, most have prepared a simple document that describes how to keep accurate records. Be sure to ask for it when you apply for a checking account.

Why should I bother with a checking account?

There are some pretty sound advantages to having a checking account. For example:

☞ With a checking account, you have as much cash as you need right in the form of a check. If you need ten dollars you can write a ten dollar check.

☞ A check is also a written record of what you spent—there can never be any doubt as the check represents proof of payment or purchase.

☞ Chances are you will be using a checking account when you grow older so why not get an early start and learn about taking care of your own finances.

There are also a few disadvantages that you should keep in mind:

☞ If you aren't sure how much money you have in your checking account (on deposit at the bank) it's not very wise to write a check—it may bounce. Bounced checks sometimes lead to misunderstandings, confusion and resentments. So do keep reasonably accurate records. Moreover, a bounced check messes up everyone's records—not just yours.

☞ Some stores or places of business won't accept a personal check in payment of goods, so your check won't be automatically welcome everywhere. And, sad to say, your local movie or video center generally deals only in cash.

7

How to Make Your Money Grow

It would all be so easy if you could just plant some loose change like you plant corn and simply watch it grow and multiply. Unfortunately, no one has figured out just how to accomplish this bit of magic. Of course, the people in the Las Vegas casinos and local state lotteries are always promising great returns for your money. Alas, there are far more chances to lose than there are to win—something they never tell you about.

The idea that your money can make you more money should not, however, be quickly dismissed. There are a number of different ways that you can take your extra money or savings and have it earn you additional money. This chapter will describe how you can take even small amounts of money, say ten dollars or twenty-five dollars and make it multiply. Not necessarily by magic but slowly and surely.

How Money Earns Money

While it might seem quite basic, many people don't understand much about how money creates money. The concept of increase or the idea of interest and return on your money confuses many people. Simply put, there are institutions and companies that will pay you a sum of money, sometimes called interest or return, if you will let them use your money.

If you are willing to lend your money to a bank, they will give you a specified additional amount of money for each day, week or month that you leave your money with them. And, if you agree in advance to leave your money in the bank for six months, a year or two years, chances are that the bank will give you an even greater rate of interest (the proportion of your money that they will give to you for its use).

The most common way of making your money grow is to put it in a savings account at a bank or savings and loan institution. The bank will typically pay you a yearly interest rate of five and one-half percent of your money. If you deposit one hundred dollars and your money remains for a whole year it will earn you at least five dollars and fifty cents and perhaps a bit more depending upon the way that the bank calculates its interest. Some banks pay higher interest than others; so you might want to check what's available in your area.

Other ways to earn money with your money include investing in certificates of deposit, money market funds or even stocks and bonds in American businesses. These methods of using your money to earn money generally involve some degree of risk or possible loss, so let's examine the element or risk.

Risk and Your Money

Just as an example, let's assume that a distant relative of yours has died and left you a thousand dollars. Now that's a pretty sizeable bit of money—not an amount you would want to keep in the bottom drawer of your dresser. There are many places that you can take this money—some will keep it very, very safe and pay you modest interest. Other places will treat your money as an investment and pay you a larger return. Generally, the amount of money that you can earn with your money is influenced by the risk involved and how quickly you can get your money back.

There is virtually no risk that you will lose any of your money if you put it in a simple savings account.

The bank or savings institution has insurance that fully protects your money against any kind of loss. Even if the bank goes out of business, the federal government guarantees that you will get your money back plus whatever interest it earned. The same would be true if you purchased government savings bonds; your money would be absolutely safe from loss.

If, however, you choose to use your imaginary thousand dollars to buy shares of stock in a company or a mutual fund, the potential return on your money may be higher, but so then is the risk. If the company you invest in goes broke or suffers some big losses, you can expect that your investment will lose money as the value of your stocks decline. Not only will you suffer a loss in some (or all) of the money you invested, you will also not earn any dividends or return on your money.

Investing in a mutual fund also has its risks. If the stocks or bonds purchased and held by a mutual fund decline, so does the value of your investment.

How much risk you wish to expose your money to is up to you. If you feel better playing it very safe, try a simple savings account, time deposit (you agree to leave your money in the bank for a specified period such as six months or a year), or government savings bond. Those of you who like an element of chance or risk can invest in any number of financial opportunities.

A Small Word of Advice

Before you turn your money over to someone else, for whatever reason, do get some objective or independent advice. If your Uncle Harry shows up at your door fresh from Alaska with a great opportunity for you to invest in his newly discovered gold mine, don't ask *him* if the investment is a good one, best to ask someone else: a teacher, banker or knowledgeable friend of the family. A little caution can save you a great deal of money. It may seem embarrassing to seek out the advice of others, but it's a good bit less embarrassing than explaining to others how you lost your money. As always (and unfortunately) "a fool and his money are soon parted."

Remember, your objective is to make your money grow, not disappear. If, however, you enjoy the excitement of high risk and high return, forget about safety and security, they are seldom seen together.

8

Red Tape and Paperwork

One of the things that mankind does very well, so it seems, is to make up rules, regulations and laws. And just to make life even more difficult, the people who give us all these rules have devised all sorts of forms, applications and agreements that must be filled out. Nobody really likes any of this but so far no great genius has figured out how we can eliminate all of this bothersome paperwork.

Many people do their best to avoid or ignore all of the rules and regulations. Like them, you may be tempted to resist all of the regulations and senseless paperwork of life. However, most of those who have tried this approach before you have finally found that it's not worth all of the effort it eventually takes to sort out the tangle. You will encounter fewer problems by simply following the rules and regulations, no matter how stupid or dumb they appear to be.

It certainly doesn't pay to drive around without a driver's license or to ignore state and federal income taxes. And it's not very wise to lie about your age so that you can work in a place where liquor is served or where the law forbids minors to work.

While it may seem strange, some of these bothersome regulations and rules are for your protection. There are laws protecting young people from being cruelly cheated out of their money by crooked merchants or from being paid an hourly pay that is below the lawful minimum wage. In order to be protected or to have your rights recognized, or merely to get a part-time job, you may be asked to fill out all sorts of forms and documents. You might just as well smile and start writing. Remember, you're not alone; everyone has to do it.

Social Security and Working Papers

Probably two of the earliest documents that you will come in contact with will be applications for a Social Security card and for working papers. These items aren't essential if you are earning money baby-sitting or mowing neighborhood lawns, but if you apply for a part-time or full-time job with any kind of company or organization you will be required to present one and possibly both documents.

Obtaining a Social Security Card

To obtain an application for a Social Security card, call or visit the nearest Social Security Administration office. They are a branch of the federal government and have many offices. When you have filled out the application according to the directions, you can return the completed application to the Social Security Administration office along with:

☞ your birth certificate

☞ personal identification such as a driver's license or school identification card so that you can prove who you are.

It doesn't cost anything to get the card, which will include an identification number. This number is yours for the rest of your life and you will be asked for it all through your life. You have just been issued your identity number by your government. If you ever lose your card, you can easily obtain a duplicate.

Your Social Security card serves a number of purposes:

☞ Your identity number is used by the government to keep a record of the amounts of money you contribute over your lifetime to the Federal Insurance Contribution Act. This is a form of insurance that you can collect when you retire.

☞ Your identity number is used by banks and other financial institutions to report your interest and dividends.

☞ Your identity number is used by the Internal Revenue Service and state tax office as your official taxpayer identity number. They use your number as a means of keeping track of all your weekly, monthly and yearly tax payments.

☞ Your identity number is used by your boss so that you are properly credited for the taxes he withheld from your pay.

☞ Your identity number is used by health insurance companies and doctors as your official control number.

Obtaining Working Papers

Many, but not all states may require that minors (under eighteen) have a work permit. You can obtain work permit applications at your local school or at any state labor department office. When you obtain a work permit application you must fill out part of it and then:

☞ your parents must give their consent, usually in writing

☞ your prospective employer will have to fill in part of the work permit application.

There are different kinds of work permits because different states have different rules. Most states will require that you show them proof of your age, usually with a birth certificate or a baptismal record. For exact details it is best to inquire at your school guidance counselor's office.

Working papers are a form of protection. They assist state governments in their guardian efforts to ensure that you are not allowed to work in dangerous or unhealthy working conditions or in places that are not considered appropriate for young people, such as barrooms and taverns. The states can also monitor your employer to make sure that he pays you at least the minimum wage.

Paying Taxes

No one really enjoys having to pay taxes. And somehow the thought of having money withheld from your small part-time or summer job paycheck really stings. You might just as well get used to it because your federal government is going to be a silent partner in all your money-earning ventures. They want what monies are legally due them and they will go to great lengths to make sure that you keep up with their tax payment requirements. There is no escape.

When you obtain a part-time or full-time job, your employer will ask that you fill out a W-4 form. This is the standard Employee's Withholding Allowance Certificate. It permits the employer to deduct, in advance, from your weekly pay the appropriate federal, state and local taxes, along with the Social Security (FICA) contribution. Your employer is directed by the various government agencies to withhold these taxes by law. How much is deducted depends upon your status and how much you expect to earn. It also depends upon how many people depend upon you for their support. As a minor, you will probably have only one allowance or dependent to declare—yourself.

In some instances you may not be required to pay any income taxes (you are exempt). If you earn during the course of a calendar year only a small sum of money—just a few hundred dollars—you may request that no taxes be withheld. Since tax laws change every year, be sure to ask about this exemption rule.

If you do have taxes withheld from your weekly paycheck, you will be required to file an income tax statement (return) at the end of the year. This needn't be all pain because many young people are entitled to a refund because of their limited earnings. The government tax return form is a simple and short one. Moreover, to assist you, your employer must provide you with a W-2 form (Wage and Tax Statement) that summarizes all the tax monies that were withheld in your name. This document is a record of your taxes. One copy must be sent to the government with your tax return.

If you are uncertain about how to fill out the income tax return, ask your parents or inquire at any Internal Revenue Service office—the government maintains plenty of them. Just remember, you will not get a tax refund (if you qualify for one) unless you file a tax return. The government is very funny that way—they expect you to notify them that they owe you money.

Major Purchases as a Minor

As mentioned earlier, most states have very specific laws that deal with the rights of minors (under eighteen) in transactions for goods and services. The laws have been developed with the idea of protecting young people from the sharp and deceitful practices of unscrupulous businessmen. The laws acknowledge that minors may be very intelligent in many areas but not sufficiently seasoned to recognize or understand a bad deal. To cite an example, a sixteen-year-old high school student has worked hard and saved his money for his first car. He goes to the Shady Motor Car Company where a high-pressure salesman sells him a very defective automobile. The sale can be voided, the car returned and the money refunded if the young man complains. Another illustration might be the seventeen-year-old girl who is dazzled by a young and attractive magazine salesman. She signs a contract to pay one hundred dollars over the period of a year for a group of magazines and gives the salesman a twenty dollar deposit. If she so desires, she can get all of her deposit refunded and void the contract. Individual states have enacted a whole series of laws to protect minors. Many consumer protection bureaus stand ready to provide assistance and directly intervene on behalf of a minor who has been too impetuous or blind to the realities of a specific purchase or contract.

Most businesses understand about the laws regarding minors and generally deal in full faith. Moreover, where there are large sums of money involved— particularly those which include an installment contract (pay so much each month)—the sellers will request that any sales agreement be signed by a parent, adult relative or guardian. Adults who act in this capacity are generally called guarantors or cosigners. Their signature fulfills two roles:

1. It makes the transaction legal and binding.

2. Their signature establishes them as legally responsible for completing the terms of the agreement if the minor can't make the payments or fulfill his or her obligations.

In other words, if you buy a car on the installment plan and your folks cosign the financial agreement, they are legally bound to make the payments if you cannot. The best way to avoid all of the issues discussed above is to follow some simple steps:

1. Be aware that some people will try to separate you from your money by deceitful or illegal practices.

2. Think carefully before you give anyone large amounts of cash. If the seller is peddling new stereo sets from the back of a truck at a very low price, common sense should warn you that once your money is gone, it's really gone. Shop at reputable stores.

3. Before any large or meaningful expenditure, ask advice and guidance.

9

Money Does Funny Things to People

People handle their money in many different ways. If you haven't noticed this fact, just watch some of your school friends or relatives for a few days. How young people approach money and spend it is largely the result of what they learn about money from their parents, brothers, sisters and relatives during their early years. As a result, some people grow up with some pretty strange ideas about the value of money and how to use it, while others seem to have a natural common sense in their management of money. At one time or another you have surely seen the person who spends his or her entire weekly allowance the first day—or maybe just gambles it all away.

Reckless spending and gambling are just two of the many ways that money can be misused and abused. And since early attitudes and habits tend to stick with people for many years—if not a lifetime—it's a pretty good idea to gain some understanding of how money affects people and how you can avoid some of the problems a poor approach to money might cause.

The Importance of Money

How important money is to a person can sometimes be difficult to determine. Often, however, people clearly communicate their feelings about the special value they place on money. Let's take some simple examples:

☞ Jeff is constantly losing money, it literally falls out of his pockets and he sometimes forgets to bring his money when he goes to a movie or for a snack.

☞ Linda loves to spend money. It slips right through her fingers whenever she has any. And she likes to call attention to how much she spends and for what items.

☞ Frank has trouble spending any money. He is not generous or easy in his approach to money. He won't lend money and he argues over a few pennies at the local McDonald's. He's generally too concerned about how much everything costs to enjoy what he buys.

Each of these ways of dealing with money is pretty obvious. Each approach signals how important money is and how it is used by people to express what they feel. There is nothing particularly wrong with these sorts of behavior unless they are carried to extremes and begin to seriously influence what you do, where you go and how you treat your friends and perhaps brothers or sisters. Of course, it's somewhat different if you are mostly broke or have very limited funds, because there just isn't much money at home. Your problem may be learning how to get along on too little or where to find a part-time job that will get you out of personal poverty. Not surprisingly, money often takes on extra importance when you don't have any. Being serious and concerned about your money (or lack of it) is fairly common. But being fixated, indifferent or consistently reckless or miserly, can lead to problems— maybe soon or maybe later.

Early Patterns

Money, physically, is nothing more than small pieces of paper and small round metal disks. However, in people's minds it takes on all sorts of meanings. To some people money represents security, popularity, independence, excitement, trouble and many other things. It really isn't the money, it's what we learned about money from those around us—primarily our parents and close relatives.

Some people grow up watching their parents struggle along with too little money or perhaps they hear too many bitter or unkind arguments between their parents—always about money. How your parents treated money and the importance they gave it will have a powerful influence on your attitudes toward money and what you do with it. Their influence can be positive or negative. For some, too much poverty might lead them to become spendthrifts whenever they have anything to spend. Constant family arguments about money might also cause some people to value money too much and become junior Scrooges or Midases.

Some young people have a rough time when they discover that their parents and the world are not standing by with an ever-ready supply. Sometimes, the great parental money machine malfunctions or becomes stubborn just when it is most needed. This may be the parents' clever way of saying that there are limits. If and when this happens to you, it's best to consider sitting down and talking with your parents about your needs.

Money isn't everything though, so when you notice your friends or relatives acting strange or unusual about money, try to keep in mind that:

☞ How people behave about their money, or lack of it, is just one aspect of their personality. People can be warm, wonderful and faithful even though they may have some miserable ideas about money.

☞ As people grow older they generally become more set in their habits and less flexible—particularly when it comes to money matters.

☞ It's much easier for people to change their attitudes toward money when they are young—a little awareness and willingness to consider other ways of looking at money and using money can go a long way.

Using and Abusing Money

Mankind has designed some pretty enjoyable and exciting ways to pry you loose from your nickels, dimes and dollars. Fortunately, most people understand that they have to be fairly disciplined about how they spend their money—largely because they only have so much available to them each week. There are, unfortunately, some people, young and old, who have real trouble understanding this. Perhaps they have other problems as well and use money unhealthily in dealing with them. Much as some fat people go on eating binges, some people go on reckless spending or gambling sprees.

One way of abusing money is to spend it all as soon as you get it. An example would be to buy something expensive for yourself just before Christmas so that you don't have any money left to buy presents for your family and friends. Gambling has also become another popular way to maintain a continuous life of self-imposed poverty. Not just the once-in-a-while card game or lottery ticket purchase but a consistent or compulsive wagering, usually involving all one's money, and even money borrowed from others. For these people their money controls them, they don't control their money.

There's also a reverse side to the coin. Among your friends and relatives there are probably a few misers who so value money that concern about spending and not having enough (and for them there never is enough) disrupts their enjoyment of life and seriously affects their relationships with most people. Their need to be in charge of their expenditures or to hold onto their money limits their fun or just plain ruins it.

In addition to the spendthrift, the gambler and the miser, there are all sorts or people with some odd but not necessarily destructive ways of handling their money. They certainly make life interesting and different.

Learning *How to Be Responsible about Your Money*

The notion of being responsible about your money may seem unusual. Of course, you personally are always sensible and careful with your funds (what little there are). Well, now that you have read through this chapter, maybe you have become aware of the fact that your ways of approaching or using money aren't all that terrific. Or perhaps you have a friend or two who could use a bit of guidance about the way they handle money.

Unfortunately, there are few, if any, schools or organizations offering practical workshops on a common sense approach to money. Too bad it has to be left to chance, luck or limited parental input, particularly during the all-important early years when habits and attitudes get formed.

Apart from reading this book for its general guidance, there *are* a few other steps you can take if you would like to improve how you feel about money, look after your finances or spend your allowance.

1. Discuss your money problems with your parents. While this may seem to be a natural first step, some young people overlook this potential source of help because they feel that their parents will be unresponsive or of little help. You won't really know unless you make the effort.

2. If your parents are unable to give you some pretty good answers, why not look to one of your teachers for some guidance.

3. School friends or personal friends who seem to have a pretty sensible approach to money can also prove helpful.

4. A family friend, relative or someone you admire and respect for their sensitivity and common sense might be of real assistance to you.

5. You can inquire at your local "hotline" or information and referral agency to see if they have any workshops, seminars or lectures on sensible money management. Don't be concerned about the fact that the sessions might be geared to adults—they have the same problems as young people, only the circumstances and amounts are different.

6. If you—or someone you know—has a compulsive gambling or spending problem—one that is making life miserable—do inquire about debt clinics, Debtors Anonymous or Gambler's Anonymous. These groups are very effective in providing aid to people with serious money problems. They don't lend money, but they do provide support and help for people who wish to change their bad habits.

10

Borrowing and Lending Money

It's probably an unusual person who has never borrowed money. At one time or another, just about everybody gets caught short or runs out of allowance too soon. And it's so easy to turn to a brother, sister, friend or parent and ask to borrow the amount you need. The chances are that no one thinks very much about the transaction, and the borrowed money is returned in a few days or so. It seems a nice, easy way to get through life, and for most people there is never much hassle or concern. However, there can be some difficulties attached to borrowing and lending money. And in these situations, a little caution and knowledge can be helpful.

Some people have been known to leave town under cover of darkness when their debts get too large. And when it comes to collecting money owed, it's not unknown for people to hire heavy-muscled, unfriendly types who enjoy breaking bones. Now, none of this may have anything to do with you now or in the future, but the pointers and hints in this chapter can help keep the borrowing and lending part of your life simple and friendly.

Simple Borrowing

There is absolutely nothing wrong with borrowing money. People and businesses do it every day. Chances are your parents borrowed money to buy the family car or home. And millions of people borrow money to fix up their home, take a vacation trip or to pay for unexpected medical bills or a college education. At the day-to-day level, small amounts of money—ten dollars, five dollars, two dollars are borrowed every day to meet sudden emergencies or take advantage of a special price offer.

In any small-scale borrowing situation there are a couple of very important assumptions involving trust and belief. They are:

1. The one lending the money believes that all of the money will be repayed to him/her

2. The lender (the one who lends the money) expects to get the money back in a reasonable amount of time.

3. The person borrowing the money represents himself/herself as reliable and ready and willing to repay the borrowed money.

4. The lender does not want to have to badger or ask the borrower for repayment.

There is one other very essential detail that is often overlooked when money is borrowed and it often creates problems when it is overlooked. Establish a definite time or date of repayment. Whether you are a lender or a borrower, it is important that there is some kind of agreement or understanding about when the money will be repaid.

When adults and businesses borrow money from banks, they usually set the terms of repayment and sign an agreement that binds them to make the payments as agreed. If you buy something like an automobile or a stereo set and pay for it in installments (so much a month), you are really borrowing money from the seller of the product. And you will have to agree to when and how much you will repay. While sellers are trusting, they also see the necessity of establishing a specific payment time.

Now, you may say what has all this got to do with borrowing ten dollars from your brother or best friend or fifty dollars from your parents for something special. An agreement about when you will repay the money does something very essential; it helps everyone avoid misunderstandings, which can often lead to hurt feelings, resentments and distrust. Needless to say, if you make an agreement to repay your best friend on Monday—try your very best to stick to your agreement. Prompt repayment is both a sign of respect and a way of saying thanks.

What to Do When You Are Having Trouble Repaying What You Borrowed

If you suddenly, or not so suddenly, discover that you won't be able to pay a loan on the agreed date, what should you do? Well it's not a popular problem to face but here are a few things you should try not to do:

☞ Desperately avoiding the person you must repay by crossing streets, ducking around corners and looking the other way will confuse or irritate any friend, not just one who was kind enough to lend you money.

☞ Getting angry at the person who lent you money simply because you can't repay him or her as you agreed isn't a good idea, especially if that person happens to be a parent.

☞ Borrowing money from Jim to pay Jack isn't a wise approach either because you are still in debt to somebody.

☞ Gambling your last few dollars, whether it be at cards or the local lottery, probably won't solve your problem, and is more likely to leave you with empty pockets.

The simplest approach, unfortunately, requires a little courage. When you can't repay as scheduled, tell the lender. By doing so, you reduce the possibility of a misunderstanding, you don't have to engage in strange behavior, and chances are you will prevent hard feelings from arising. You may be a bit embarrassed about admitting you can't repay on schedule and don't be surprised if you feel a bit defensive about it all; these are natural reactions. Once you have notified the lender, be prepared to discuss or suggest a new payment date. Choose one that is more reasonable and gives you ample time to get the money.

Probably the least acceptable solution to the problem is to ignore repayment by pretending no debt exists. Such action doesn't lead to very happy endings. It's a good way to lose friends and exasperate relatives. Remember, you agreed to pay back the loan. It's all about learning to be trustworthy and honoring your agreements.

Borrowing Too Often or Too Much

Sometimes people find themselves running short of money every week or every month so they borrow liberally from friends, relatives or acquaintances. You already know this isn't the best approach to chronic shortages of money. Since few people like to play bank, no matter how much they love you, if you find yourself in this predicament, perhaps you should look at the size of your allowance, how you spend (or overspend) your money, and consider the possibility of establishing some simple money management rules for yourself. Continuous borrowing may strain friendships as well as reduce your own sense of responsibility. All in all, it's not a great way to go through life.

Borrowing more than you really need may appear to be harmless but it isn't always. Since you are going to have to pay it back, why bother with more than you need? One thing for sure, there are plenty of temptations and ways of spending the extra money. Extra money has a way of disappearing almost magically. So if you don't need it, try to avoid the temptation.

Where to Borrow

While this may seem like a novel idea, you should consider carefully the person from whom you intend to borrow. For example, it's not too wise to attempt to borrow from anyone who:

☞ worries a lot about money and is still holding on to the first dollar he or she earned. Insecure people tend to make you sorry that you ever borrowed from them.

☞ is on such a very tight and limited budget that if you don't repay promptly it will be a real hardship for them. In other words don't take someone's last dollar no matter how lovingly it is offered.

☞ you already owe money to. It is easy to run up a sizeable debt that you won't be able to repay fully for a year.

If you need a fairly large sum, it's best to consider borrowing from someone who is reliable and won't request that you repay early. It also helps if your source has money to spare. Parents are probably the most reliable source for this. However, if you have trouble repaying loans, think twice about borrowing from parents or just think twice about borrowing!

Advice to a Lender

If you are one of those kind souls or good samaritans who is free and relaxed about lending money to friends, relatives or acquaintances, the chances are you will be more popular and welcome than the nonlenders of this world. And in all likelihood, most of your lending experiences will be pleasant with pretty prompt return of your money. However, to avoid those rare instances where a loan goes sour, you might wish to keep in mind the following thoughts.

☞ Don't press "extra" money on a borrower. If the person asks for five dollars don't insist upon lending ten dollars.

☞ If you have very limited funds, don't go broke by making a loan.

☞ If the borrower is uncertain how much he or she wants, don't volunteer an amount, ask: "How much do you need?"

☞ Establish a repayment date such as "a week from today."

☞ On repayment day, or any day after that, it is absolutely all right to ask the borrower about your money. Don't be bashful or hesitant. But try to do it in a pleasant, quiet manner. There is nothing wrong with being quietly persistent.

☞ If asked, be willing to extend the repayment time, but do agree on another date that's reasonable. Request part payment if you need it.

☞ If you have trouble collecting on a loan, don't lend money to the person again. Try not to get angry or resentful, just keep in mind that some people just don't know how to be responsible and reliable about money. (They probably haven't read this book.)

☞ Just because it's a small sum you lent doesn't mean you should overlook nonrepayment.

Unfortunately, a book can't teach you the most important lesson of all: You don't *have* to lend money—even when you are being pressed hard. While you may feel a bit guilty or stingy, it's perfectly sound judgement to say "sorry, no" whenever you want to say "no" and it's especially all right to say "no" when your instincts or little inner voice warns you that the loan may lead to problems.

11

Cashless Money

Most young people use cash money for whatever it is they buy. There's nothing wrong with straight cash transactions; in fact, most businesses would be overjoyed if all of their customers paid with cash. It would save them a great deal of paperwork, adjustment and collection problems. As young people reach their mid-teens and late teens, however, they begin to see the advantages of using "cashless money" for many of their purchases of goods and services, and most of them will continue to use cashless money throughout their adult years. This chapter briefly describes what cashless money is all about, how it works and the privileges and problems that go along with using cashless money.

What Is Cashless Money?

There are any number of ways to buy goods and services without giving the seller actual cash money. Instead of cash, people make their purchases using some kind of document that "represents" real cash money. A few simple examples will help make it all clear for you.

☞ Your mother goes to the local department store and buys some towels and bed linens. Instead of handing the clerk cash for the merchandise she presents a store charge card. Her purchases are recorded along with her card number on a special form. The clerk returns the store charge card to your mother and hands her the merchandise. No cash was used but your mother purchased some household necessities.

☞ You go away on a vacation trip in the family car. You notice that your father pays for the gas with an oil company credit card—the station attendant merely records the purchase amount, the credit card number, and obtains your father's signature. Again no cash was used. You also notice that your father paid the motel charge with his American Express card. Once again, the card represented cash to the motel owner and he went through the same procedure as the gas station attendant.

☞ Your parents generously offer to buy your first car for you. Once you have selected the car you like, your father gives the automobile dealer a personal check for the cost of the car. In this instance, your father didn't have to carry thousands of dollars in cash to the car dealer. His personal check represented cash payment.

In each of the above instances, a plastic credit card or a simple personal check form readily represented cash. Naturally, at some point in the near future, your mother will have to pay the department store and your father will have to forward payment to the oil company and the American Express Company.

Why Bother with Anything but Cash?

To some people, the idea of getting involved in cashless living may seem like a lot of bother and headaches. They may bring up such painful and time-consuming inconveniences as:

☞ Visiting a bank and filling out all of the application forms required to open a checking account.

☞ Trudging around to each major department store to request their application form and inquiring about the eligibility and restrictions regarding young people being issued a store charge card.

☞ Sending away a request for an application to a general purpose credit card such as American Express, or a bank credit card such as MasterCard or Visa.

☞ Keeping personal records of your use of a checking account, store charge card or bank credit card. Each month you will have to match your expenditures with the monthly charge or activity statement sent to you by a bank, department store or credit card firm.

Certainly none of these activities are particularly appealing. And just to add to the difficulties, if you are under a certain age, you may be required to have a parent or guardian cosign or guarantee payment of any charges that you incur. You probably won't be prohibited from obtaining a store charge card or American Express card—it's just that there will probably be special conditions involved until you reach eighteen or twenty-one years of age. The conditions aren't restrictive or discriminatory, they just protect the store or credit card company against loss by reason of nonpayment. Just as drinking and driving don't mix well, young people and charge cards can sometimes cause problems that are difficult to untangle.

The Advantages of Cashless Money

While there may appear to be some pretty good arguments why you shouldn't bother with cashless money, there are also some pretty sound advantages to cashless money including the following:

☞ You don't need to carry much cash around with you, especially large amounts.

☞ You don't have to worry about losing your cash or being robbed of it.

☞ You will receive a written record of your purchases or payments. Banks, credit card firms and stores all send you a monthly statement of your activities, usually with some kind of copy of each of your transactions.

☞ You will have much greater convenience with cashless money. If you see something on sale or at a special price and you don't have enough cash with you, you can buy it and pay by check or with a store charge card, bank card or credit card.

☞ You actually pay for your purchases sometime in the future. The "buy now-pay later" privilege may even include the opportunity to pay for a purchase over a period of months. This arrangement is often known as extended payment, installment credit or revolving credit.

Major Forms of Cashless Money

Most adults use one or more of three major forms of cashless money in their everyday living. They are:

1. A checking account. Checking accounts are probably the most frequently used form of cashless money. Instead of paying for goods and services with cash, a simple personal check completes the transaction. And, always, your returned check (sent to you by the bank after it has been cashed) is your proof of payment should a dispute over payment ever arise.

2. Store charge accounts. Purchasing what you want with a store charge card can be a convenient way to shop. The store recognizes you as a valuable, reliable customer and allows you to purchase and take merchandise by merely presenting your personal store charge card. Naturally, the card is only good for use in the store issuing you the card.

3. Bank charge cards and general purpose credit cards. These cards allow the cardholder the privilege of obtaining goods and services at many different kinds of businesses or establishments all across the nation or even the world. A MasterCard is accepted by thousands of stores, hotels, restaurants, recreation areas and mail order firms. General purpose credit cards

such as American Express are also honored at thousands of places. These cards are particularly convenient when you are traveling and don't like the idea of carrying a large amount of cash.

Privileges and Problems

While it's convenient and often sensible to have a charge account, checking account or charge card, these privileges also involve some simple responsibilities. While you personally may not be legally bound to pay for anything you obtained with a charge account or credit card (in most states you may not be financially accountable until you are eighteen or twenty-one), someone in your family will have to pay the bill— usually whichever family member acted as cosigner or guarantor of your repayment. If, and when, you decide that you want a store charge account or charge card, be prepared to meet the simple obligation of paying for what you ordered. However, if your parents get a card for you and are willing to pay for all your purchases— enjoy it, but try not to take advantage of it.

12

Getting More Money
for Yourself

You can readily expect that as you grow, so will your
needs—not the least of which will probably be your
need for more money. There will be plenty of occasions when you wish that you had more money to
spend or when you need more money just to get
through the week. Once it becomes painfully clear that

your present allowance or income isn't making it for you, you should start looking into the ways and means of getting more money.

Probably the first issue to consider is "When should I try to get more money?" Perhaps the best answer is:

☞ When you need it.

☞ When you feel you deserve it.

☞ When you want it—for whatever reason.

☞ When the timing and circumstances are most favorable.

Just because you are seeking more money however doesn't mean that you will always succeed. But with a bit of careful thought and planning, you can increase your chances.

Approaching Your Parents for More Money

A little strategy and a timely approach can work wonders. Some of the practical steps that you can take to increase your chances of success are:

1. Make a list of all your expenses, particularly all of the essential ones. Discuss with your parents the specific items that your allowance is supposed to cover and how it doesn't or almost

doesn't make it. Carefully explain how you have examined your weekly needs and why the money you receive doesn't meet your needs. Be ready to show examples. If you are expecting an increase in your expenses in the near future —especially when starting a new school year— show on paper how your new needs will put you in the proverbial poorhouse.

2. Speak with your friends and find out what kind of weekly allowances or income they receive or need per week. Be sure to inquire among friends who have family circumstances similar to yours. While it might be a clever idea to ask only friends with very rich parents, your parents may catch on to your strange fact-finding system. Once you have made a list of your friends' allowances or expenditures, present it to your parents. Most parents want to be fair in their allocation to their children. They just don't know how to keep current on allowances and expenses. So, help them become knowledgeable—unless, of course, you discover that your allowance is already greater than that of most of your friends!

3. There's nothing wrong with asking for a bit more than you absolutely need—especially if you expect your parents might do a little bargaining or trimming of your request. Most likely, you will soon be needing that extra margin of money.

4. If your parent's reaction to your request is one of strong resistance, if you are met with words like "no way," "ask us next year," or "you've got to be kidding," then you may have to use some really persuasive tactics. Be ready and willing to suggest that you will take on added family chores or special tasks. In this way you can honestly claim that you are "earning" the additional money. It helps to have in your mind a small but meaningful list of chores that you are willing to bargain about. Preferably chores that your parents dislike intensely—so they are more receptive to your offer.

5. Timing is an important element. Wait until you find your parents in a warm, happy or responsive mood. When your mother or father announces that he or she got a raise, made some extra money or received a tax refund is probably a favorable time. It's not too wise to make your request just after your parents finished a heated argument over money or your father announces that his firm is going bankrupt. Quite often, good timing can mean the difference between success and failure—especially when it is coupled with a sincere presentation of some simple but telling facts.

6. Try not to ask for increases too often. Perhaps no more than once every six months or once a year. If you cry poor too often, you will lose some of the persuasive impact and your facts

probably won't have changed much in your favor over shorter periods of time.

Pricing Your Services

Whether you personally offer your services to others or are employed by a company, there are some tactics that can help you get a reasonable return for your services.

1. WORKING FOR YOURSELF

If you offer your services in your neighborhood shoveling snow, babysitting, mowing lawns or helping shut-ins it should result in a fair or reasonable return of money for your efforts.

☞ Always inquire around about the going rate others may be charging for the same or similar services.

☞ Where you know you can do well, ask for a little more than the going rate. If there is no known rate, and it is something you can do well, try not to offer your services for less than the minimum wage (about three dollars and forty cents per hour).

☞ If the prospect resists your price, suggest something extra that you will do to make your price more attractive, such as doing the dishes while

babysitting or fertilizing the grass after mowing
and raking.

☞ Consider the ability of the prospect to pay and
the extent of the competition. If you are the only
person willing to babysit on New Year's Eve or
the only young man in the neighborhood with a
shovel and a willingness to dig out cars after a
blizzard—ask for more money. If your customers
live in a mansion—ask for more than you might
ask a poor old widow.

2. WORKING FOR OTHERS

When you work for others, say at a McDonald's or at a
car wash, things are a bit different. Your employer or
future boss will generally tell you how much he is
willing to pay for your services. That doesn't mean you
can't ask for more, it merely means that a wage has
generally been set. You can certainly ask for more
whenever you wish. Some of the above guidelines also
apply here such as:

☞ Be sure to ask the beginning salary and compare
it with the prices paid for similar work at other
companies. You may find that different restaurants, stores or car washes pay substantially different wages.

☞ It's best to ask for more money just after you have
done some exceptional work or have just been
praised.

☞   Don't ask for more money if your boss has a hangover, is in a mean mood or has just requested a loan from the bank. Timing is always very important.

☞   Do inquire about how frequently the firm gives raises (every six months, etc.) and how often you will have a job performance review that can lead to a raise. Keep in mind that it's perfectly natural to want more money for the work you do—most people do. Don't feel awkward or hesitant about inquiring or requesting an increase.

When Not to Ask for More Money

Sometimes the conditions or circumstances may be such that you should delay or postpone asking for more money. As mentioned earlier, requesting a bigger allowance right on the heels of a huge parental argument about money is not a very wise action. Your chances of failure are pretty high—just as they would be if you approached your boss during his worst sales week in a year. Waiting for an opportune time isn't easy and some people just aren't easy to approach, so you have to be patient and wait for those moments when they appear content or reasonably civil rather than grim and sour. Don't forget to have your lines (request) memorized and your supporting reasons and facts at your fingertips. It also helps not to request a raise right after your coworker asked your boss or your brother just asked your parents—leave a little breathing room for everyone to recover. The idea is always to strike when the time is right or conditions are most favorable. Try not to be intimidated or of faint heart. Stay alert and keep looking for an opening.

13

Your Money and Your Future

Few people of any age show much interest in planning, organizing or thinking ahead about their life. There's even more resistance to such activity among young people. And it's certainly understandable since so much of their early years is directed and controlled by forces outside themselves—parents, relatives, teachers, doctors and many others. And when they do look into a piece of their future, they usually see more of the same—school, summer work and life at home. It's sometimes pretty difficult to see how money, future planning and today's actions have anything to do with each other. Yet they are all linked. And what you learn about managing your money today will have a great deal of impact on your life later on.

Your parents understand this. For example, if your family has limited financial means and you want to go to college or trade school, some planning and managing of money has to be done. Sitting down and putting plans on paper, figuring out what amounts of money are involved and organizing how to get it are all part of being responsible. And since you will be expected to take charge of your money all your life, it's not a bad idea to begin to plan for investing in yourself and your future.

Doing Some Planning

The thought of making plans involving your future is certainly frightening, especially for those unfortunate ones among you who can't make it to next week's allowance without three days of empty pockets. But some parts of your life can benefit from even a little advance planning. Most parents take time to plan for a summer vacation, and part of their planning activity involves estimating the cost of the vacation and how they will get the money needed. Everybody does some kind of planning, even if they don't know that it's called by that name. When you ask for or buy something that's to be used in another season—such as water skis in March—you are taking action now so that you will have what you need in the future.

There are two very simple kinds of planning:

Short Term—covers the near future—the next few months.

Long Term—covers a longer period from three to five years.

Short-term planning might consist of looking for a suitable present for your father's birthday, which will occur next month, or perhaps seeking a summer job during spring vacation. Long-term planning may appear to cover a big stretch of time, but some important things will probably be happening to you during these years such as:

☞ Going on to college or technical/trade school

☞ Getting a job, perhaps a part-time job or two while still in high school and then a full-time job in a field you like

☞ Leaving home, getting your own apartment, possibly getting married

Some people have trouble understanding that if a person doesn't make some decisions about what to do with their life, not much happens. And if they do make some decisions, they can only get there by planning and taking some actions. For example, if you want to go away to tennis school, which your parents can't afford for you, the chances are pretty good that you won't get there without a work plan and a saving program. Making things happen takes a bit more than just wishful thinking. It involves taking charge of your life.

There are, however, some fairly easy ways to start planning:

1. Think about what it is that you want in the next few years, a job, more education or training, a car, a new stereo system. Write them down on paper.

2. Ask yourself who is really responsible for getting what you want. Maybe it's you alone, or a cooperative effort with your parents—or someone else.

3. Now list next to each item you want what steps, actions and efforts will be required to get it. Usually, it will involve money—so estimate the cost, the amount of time it may take and who is responsible for getting the money.

4. If it involves you and money, start developing a plan or working on the actions you will have to take—such as putting aside a dollar a week or getting a part-time job.

Investing in Yourself

How you decide to run your life is pretty much up to you—probably with some strong suggestions from your parents and other relatives. And if you are like most people, you want your life to be exciting, enjoyable, rewarding, prosperous and secure. One way to get what you want out of life is to invest in yourself. That may sound like a pretty strange concept, since most people invest in stocks, bonds or real estate, but think about it. Why not try treating yourself as an important investment. To have a full, wonderful life often means developing skills and know-how, learning about people and business. Though it may seem strange, you can positively influence your future right now, today! Here are just a few ways that you can start investing in yourself.

☞ You can ask advice about how to best reach your short-term or long-term goals. Talk about them with your parents, relatives and friends.

☞ You can study or become acquainted with the kinds of vocations that interest you most. If you are interested in nursing you can become a volunteer worker at a local hospital. If you are interested in engineering or things mechanical, try for a part-time job at a garage or construction company.

☞ You can put aside some of your money (either earned or given to you) to further your education. Maybe it's computer school or a trade school— where you might even be able to take some courses before you have completed high school.

☞ If you want to work with people selling things, try a door-to-door sales job in your spare time and then take some local courses in selling.

What you have to invest is your time, your money and your willingness to set aside a bit of today's fun for a great future. And, yes, it sometimes takes a good bit of effort and work too.

Future Schooling

You've probably heard it so many times you could cover your ears—those great words "How do you ever expect to get anywhere or have a good life if you don't have an education?" Well, many people have done quite nicely without doing very much studying or going to college or trade school. But the rather overwhelming findings from many studies are that men and women get farther in life and prosper more with additional education. This doesn't mean you have to get a four-year college education. Trade and technical schools are booming. The computer programmer and the plumber make as much as a bank vice president. But a major ingredient is some kind of additional schooling or training. And that costs money.

If you have done your best, and there just isn't enough money to get you enrolled, you can consider three major options:

1. Work full time for a year or two and save up as much as possible so that you can get back to school quickly.

2. Work full time and attend night classes. Many people have gotten advanced education this way. It's slower and takes plenty of determination as well, because people don't have as much energy or alertness after a hard day at work.

3. Obtain an educational loan from your local bank or through the school. Most schools have advisors who will explain the requirements and procedures that must be followed to get a loan. The good thing about an educational loan is that you don't have to make repayments until you have completed school and have a job.

How you obtain the money to invest in your education depends on your circumstances. If you are lucky, your parents may have put aside the money for your future. However, with the high cost of any kind of education, most parents just can't put aside enough. That puts some of the burden on you, and unless you're the class genius or football star with all sorts of scholarships waiting for you, there's a good chance that you will have to do some work and contribute to your education. You might consider some of the following as you develop a schooling plan:

☞ Start planning early. If you wait till your senior year in high school, chances are you won't be able to save much.

☞ Try to get summer jobs and part-time work during the school year.

☞ Establish some savings rules, such as putting aside one-third of what you earn or one-half of your summer job pay.

☞ Develop a definite saving schedule. Put something aside each week that you are working—or every other week.

☞ When you get money gifts on your birthday or other occasions, make an effort to set aside a certain portion of the gift.

Your Own Apartment/Home

Years ago, most young people lived with their family after completing high school, regardless of whether they went on to more schooling. They remained home because of convenience, economics and their emotional ties to the family. But living styles have changed, and many young people are leaving the family nest soon after their high school days are completed. It's quite probable that in the near future more young people will be establishing their own apartment or home while they are still in high school. Like everyone else, young people want their independence. They want to experience life without heavy parental guidance and restrictions. Unfortunately, one of the responsibilities that goes along with new independence is financial self-reliance. If a young person wants to move into an apartment or home, he or she will have to prepared to meet the money obligations involved. Each month, money must be saved to pay for the rent, electric and gas service, telephone charges and food and household supplies. Whether you are sharing a home with one or two other young people or living alone, a common sense payment plan has to be worked out. Landlords expect their money on time and the telephone and electric companies have a very harsh way of showing their displeasure if you fail to pay your charges. They simply cut off your service.

Getting a place of your own will involve some extraordinary expenses at the beginning for household furniture, linens, rugs, staples and supplies. Also, when people rent an apartment or home, it is a general business practice for the owner to require a special security deposit equal to one or two months' rent. This is kept by the owner and returned when the lease ends. Of course, if the tenant causes damage to the property or fails to pay the rent, the security deposit (or a portion of it) is kept by the owner to cover his repairs or lost rental payment.

Before you move into an apartment, sign any kind of lease, or part with any of your hard-earned money, it's always best to obtain advice and guidance. Although the laws protecting consumers have helped many people, there are still unscrupulous landlords and rental agents who might take your money illegally or disappear into the night with a good faith deposit.

Getting Married

Many young people get married while still in their teens. They feel that it's important to have the love, support and sharing of a mate while they get themselves established. Like everywhere else, financial planning and money management are important parts of marriage. It's great to be able to live on love, but landlords, utility companies and the local grocer aren't too sympathetic to people who can't pay for goods and services.

It's essential that the young couple sit down and look at their financial situation and discuss what is a workable and sensible money management plan. Some of the important questions to be asked should include:

☞ Who is going to work

☞ How much money, after taxes, will they have to live on each week

☞ If one person is attending school, will that person work part time to add to the couple's weekly income

☞ Who will pay the monthly bills

☞ How much money will be needed each month for rent (or mortgage payment), utilities, telephone, food, clothing, toiletries, medicine and medical services and car maintenance

☞ What loans have to be paid monthly (auto, furniture or personal loan)

☞ How much money can be put into weekly or monthly savings

One element that is often overlooked is called the "prudent reserve." Every family should have money put away for emergencies or personal disasters. If the husband loses his job and the wife has only a low-paying job, the couple may not be able to survive economically. An amount equal to two or three month's total financial needs should be kept in some kind of bank or easy-to-get-to money account. Tough times can happen to young people just as well as to older ones. And according to some family experts, many young marriages suffer great stresses and problems because of early financial difficulties. A little planning can reduce the problems and tensions of getting started.

14

Learning to Enjoy Your Money

Whether it's money given to you or money that you have earned, a good portion of your money should be used for your enjoyment and pleasure. One of the many ways, and an important one, that people learn to handle money is by spending some of it on something they really want. And unless you and your family are suffering from bone-chilling poverty, there ought to be a few dollars that you can set aside for your own personal—this is what I want—pleasure. You will probably hear relatives or friends tossing around plenty of reasons why you shouldn't be good to yourself. Everything from "How can you waste your money on that?" to "Put something aside for a rainy day" will probably reach your ears. But somewhere there may be other voices that you also hear. "You can't take it with you." "If you can't be good to yourself who can?" "Live a little!" "Don't be a slave to money." "Money is to be spent, not worshipped."

While you are spending some money for your own enjoyment, you should also consider sharing with others by spending a bit of your money for their benefit. You can show your appreciation and concern for others with little surprises or gifts. Buying someone a Coke or a slice of pizza is one way to share. Giving someone a small unexpected gift is a spirit booster—and it can do wonders for a romance. Another very special way to share involves giving to a special cause or an organization that you feel strongly about. Whether it is a donation to UNICEF to help starving and sick children worldwide or a dollar or so to the local athletic equipment fund; this kind of sharing helps build self appreciation as well. Sure, it may put a temporary dent in your wallet, but the knowledge that you helped someone else or supported an important group with your money creates a satisfaction of another sort.

Remember, if you don't learn how to enjoy your money when you are young, there is the very sad possibility that you may never learn how to "treat yourself and others." Since you presumably only travel this earth once, why not reward yourself and also spread a little joy to others?

Being Good to Yourself

There is probably no one so sad as people who are unable to celebrate and give to themselves. It's generally a sign that they don't think very much of themselves. Such people can easily spend money on the necessities such as lunch, carfare, school supplies, school events or perhaps for a charitable cause. They may even be pretty good about the very small rewards —a candy bar here, a movie there. But when it comes to anything of substance—a new jacket, a special bracelet, cowboy boots, a walkman radio, a set of oil paints or wall posters for their room—they just can't bring themselves to spend the money *they already have* for these items. Maybe you have heard some of their excuses or perhaps thought of them yourself. They go something like this: "I don't know, maybe I'll get it later." "I really don't need it right now—I can get by a bit longer with what I have." "Gee, I'd like to get it but it might leave me a bit short next week." "It's a nice idea but I really don't need anything that fancy, good or special."

There will always be plenty of supposedly sound and practical reasons for not treating yourself. But sometimes the best way to get special enjoyment from your money is to say to yourself: "I've got the money." "I want it (them)." "I deserve it."

Then do it, buy it, order it, subscribe to it or whatever is required. Say "yes" to yourself. Being good to yourself in a sensible way isn't self-indulgence or reckless spending—it's self-appreciation.

If you think you have difficulty "treating yourself" try to consider the following:

☞ When you are tempted or are considering buying something just because you would like it—try to turn off all the negative "you can't afford it, don't deserve it" voices in your head.

☞ Ask yourself how many times you have gotten something special just for yourself. If the answer is seldom or not at all, ask yourself "would I really enjoy this?" If the answer is "yes" read on.

☞ Assuming that you really do have enough money or can readily get it, just maybe you should say yes to yourself and go ahead and buy it. A little extra enjoyment can't really be all that bad.

Being Good to Others

People who have trouble with money often find it difficult to spend their money for the benefit of others. It's understandable. If a person can't spend money for what he or she wants, then spending money spontaneously for a friend or relative can also be troublesome. Lots of young people with limited allowances or funds grumble about buying birthday and holiday gifts, but they somehow manage to generate enough spirit of giving.

Some of the real joy comes when you can spend some of your money on a surprise gift or a small token of appreciation for someone you like or enjoy being with. Not a required giving occasion, but an impromptu "I want to do this for you because . . ." occasion. Such moments don't have to be big and splashy; a box of chocolates, a bunch of daisies, treating someone to a milkshake, a Whopper or a movie are just a few of the ways you can show another person that you care or really like them. And while it's fun and exciting to do something special for someone you are dating, try doing it for some of the other people in your life. It may require some extra work or real struggle to set aside a few dollars to pay for a treat, but it's well worth it all. Since most of your joys and good times in life will involve people, it's never too early to start recognizing people in little ways. Just think, if you enjoy little surprises, others might also.

Here are just a few ways of being good to others— maybe you can try one of them.

☞ Send someone a humorous greeting card.

☞ Bring your mother her favorite cake or pie (unless she's on a diet)

☞ Take your sister or brother to a rock concert

☞ Buy your best friend a stereo record or tape by his or her favorite group

☞ Give your father a book, maybe about "progressive and permissive child rearing"

☞ Give your grandparents a framed picture of yourself

☞ Buy your cat some catnip or your dog a favorite chewy toy

The easiest way to start being good to others is with little inexpensive gestures. It's not so much the gift but the thought and consideration that warms people's hearts. So why not celebrate those around you who love you or maybe just plain put up with you week in and week out.

Common Sense with Dollars and Cents

If you have heard it once, you have probably heard it a hundred times—"A fool and his money are soon parted." And somewhere in your life, you have probably ended up on the sour end of a bargain or deal. Maybe it was nasty deception on someone else's part or perhaps you just wanted something to be more than it was. The result was that you didn't get your money's worth or you just plain got taken.

While this book may give you some assistance in developing a sensible approach to money matters, it can't possibly provide you with a comprehensive list of the hundreds of ways that you can be unkindly or unjustly separated from your money. People of all ages generally get deceived or cheated because:

☞ They act impulsively without thinking about or doing a little investigating concerning the "bargain" or "special offer."

☞ They act alone without seeking advice or other opinions. Too often they feel foolish or too proud to get advice.

☞ They build up the special offer or item to be more than it really is. They give it magical qualities that don't exist.

☞ They recognize that the bargain is a bit risky or "funny," but they have trouble saying no to fast-talking or persuasive people.

In most money transactions the time-honored rule is still "the buyer beware." Generally, ignorance is no excuse or refuge although most states have laws to protect minors (those under sixteen or eighteen years of age) from being cheated. When it's a small amount of money that's lost, people usually don't attempt any formal complaint in small claims court or with the local consumer protection bureau. They just take their punishment silently and try to conceal their foolishness. And, that's too bad, because the thieves just keep doing business untouched by those they cheated.

When you are out there in the "marketplace" you might want to keep these suggestions in mind if you are thinking of spending some of your hard-to-come-by money.

☞ Share your purchase plans with relatives or friends, and if you are at all concerned, ask their advice.

☞ Find someone who knows about the kind of product or service you are considering and seek their guidance.

☞ Where possible, compare prices, product or service performance capabilities.

☞ If you find yourself getting so excited that you absolutely have to have it "right now," try to contain your enthusiasm and give the purchase more thought.

☞ Listen for that little voice within you that says "I don't know, something is funny about this . . ." When you hear the voice it's best to stop and get advice.

Give a Little

Throughout your life you will be getting all sorts of appeals and pleas to give some of your money to worthy causes. There will be far more requests than you can ever possibly satisfy. But this doesn't mean you should ignore them all because there are so many or because you have too little money. In simple terms, everybody has the responsibility to do what he or she can to support what is important to them. Maybe you have a favorite organization or charity, such as the Little League or the local school for the blind. Whatever it is, try to set aside a little money to help meet their needs. Or better yet, give some of your time as well as some of your money. Chances are you won't get much recognition or your name in the paper but you may feel better about yourself because you cared. Giving isn't always easy and it may seem to be pretty much one way. Unfortunately, the way life is constructed we seldom get a chance to witness the results of our giving— you can't ever see the little East African child you saved with your donation to UNICEF's trick-or-treat program or your purchase of UNICEF holiday greeting cards—but somewhere it all registers and leaves an impression.